D0184664

I'M HERE I THINK, WHERE ARE YOU?

Letters from a Touring Actor

TIMOTHY WEST

I'M HERE I THINK, WHERE ARE YOU?

Letters from a Touring Actor

Foreword by Prunella Scales

NICK HERN BOOKS
London

A Nick Hern Book

I'm Here I Think, Where Are You? first published
in 1994 by Nick Hern Books Limited.
14 Larden Road. London W3 7ST

Copyright © 1994 by Timothy West
Foreword copyright © 1994 by Prunella Scales

Timothy West has asserted his right to be identified
as the author of this work

Front cover photo by Philip Stroud

A CIP catalogue record for this book is available
from the British Library

ISBN 1 85459 222 X

Typeset by Country Setting, Woodchurch. Kent TN26 3TB
Printed and bound in Great Britain by Bath Press, Avon

CONTENTS

FOREWORD

One of the questions most often asked of married actors (just after 'However d'you learn all those words?' and shortly before 'What's it like playing a love scene with someone you hate?') is, 'How have you managed to stay together so long in a profession notorious for promiscuity and broken partnerships?'

'Prolonged and frequent separation,' we reply with lofty smiles: 'maintains your relationship at fever pitch.' (Though personally I always clutch feverishly at the nearest piece of wood as I say it.)

In fact actors married to each other often may spend more time together than couples in many other occupations, and not only when both are out of work. Rehearsal periods bring a relatively normal nine-to-five working day, while long runs often mean either or both being in for lunch, and indeed tea, before as it were leaving for the office. Of course, if the two of you are working in different media, things become more complicated: one will get up for early morning filming only four or five hours after the other comes in from the theatre, and arrive home ravenous and exhausted just as the other is setting off for work. Even if you are both lucky enough to be in West End runs at the same time, there can be difficulties. 'Come and collect me after the show and we'll go home together,' Tim would say cheerily while I was in a contemporary play at Wyndham's and he was playing Bolingbroke to Ian McKellen 's Richard II at the

Piccadilly. So when my own modest show ended, just after 10.00 p.m., I would trot dutifully round to his dressing-room, sit there for three quarters of an hour until the curtain fell and Tim had removed his wig, tights, body make-up and facial hair and had a drink, go out to supper with umpteen chums who had been in front, and totter home exhausted in the small hours of the morning, just about in time to be woken by the children.

And then there is the problem – the phenomenon – of touring. Although when our children were small we spent a good deal of time and trouble, and most of our money, joining each other on the road and taking the children with us, the touring actor's life inevitably brings weeks and indeed long months of separation. Tim was for sixteen years involved with Prospect, a theatre company devoted almost exclusively to regional and overseas touring, and although I too worked for them occasionally, and did a fair amount of touring for other managements, there were for me long stretches of time alone at home with the aforementioned offspring. The conversation of young children, however accomplished and beloved, can pall; domestic and professional stress builds up; telephone calls are expensive, frustrating, and sometimes geographically impossible, and Tim loathes the telephone anyway.

So letters become crucially important, and can even transform these times into a sort of epistolary holiday together, untrammelled by domestic preoccupations. After all, it's quite cheering to know that someone has thought long and hard enough about you to write four or five pages from such diverse and exotic locations as Ravello, the Chateau Commodore Melbourne, London Airport, Nottingham Castle, Mombasa, the Philharmonic Café Blackpool, Santa Barbara, the Free Library in Renfrew and

Madam Clark's Ale and Porter House Wolverhampton. 'Hooray, writing to you again', one of them begins, 'I do miss your letters when we're together . . '

This book is, of course, only one side of a torrid correspondence that has continued over more than thirty years – all the news that's fit to print, in fact, one way and another. Tedious domestic details have been ruthlessly deleted, and soppy or scurrilous bits reserved for later or even posthumous publication. Reading the letters over again in book form, I'm aware of a faintly melancholy feeling, as though the past were being buried instead of recalled: but I hope people will enjoy them, and laugh, and be intrigued. I love them very much, but then no doubt I'm prejudiced.

Prunella Scales
June 1994

Years ago when I was in weekly rep, we were joined for one production by an elderly actor who might best be described as being Of The Old School. He had a fine voice, a considerable stage presence, and was unfailingly courteous to all.

He had, however, one disconcerting habit. In rehearsal, when after a coffee break we resumed working on a scene from the point where we had left off, he would take up a new position absolutely centre stage, and turning to his fellow actor with an expression of avuncular solicitude, would observe: 'Let's see, I'm here, I think; where are you?'

I'M HERE I THINK, WHERE ARE YOU?

Letters from a Touring Actor

This correspondence began in 1961, before Pru and I were married. At the time I was on tour with Brian Rix's company in the farce Simple Spymen. *I was 27, and consequently had been engaged to play the elderly Intelligence Officer, Colonel Gray-Balding.*

The tour was for twenty-six weeks.

Theatre Royal
Nottingham
October 1961

We didn't play on the Monday this week, because in the afternoon the stage was needed for an ambitious Cookery Demonstration. When I arrived the place was full of trestles bearing kitchen utensils and plates of cake, an enormous gas stove stood upstage centre, and a largish orchestra was rehearsing in the pit. Men in white coats carrying pulverisers and drums of flour paced the corridors, and a large woman in a plastic apron was sitting in my dressing room checking her shopping list.

Andy Sachs and I thought we ought to see this, and managed to negotiate for two free seats. It's an entirely new form of theatre, a sort of pantomime in food. The star is a lady called Marguerite Patten, who has a television cookery programme of her own, and this is how part of the afternoon went:

Marguerite Patten is at a table, having just completed some culinary triumph involving a great deal of chocolate blancmange. She speaks loudly, scorning microphones.

A female assistant stands at a respectful distance, to hand props. This person is not an actress.

PATTEN: Now, what are we going to do with all this

Pearce Duff's Blancmange we have left over? I'll tell you. We are going to make some Pearce Duff Novelties for our Children's Party. What about some Chocolate Mice? Now I'm not very fond of mice as pets, but ·I do like Pearce Duff's Chocolate Mice, and I'm going to show you how to make them. But first of all, it's time to see how our roast pork is getting on in our Creda Cookmaster.

Prolonged business at oven. We glimpse the pork.

PATTEN: Very nicely as you see. Now to return to our chocolate rabbits. First, take a tablespoonful of your Pearce Duff Chocolate Blancmange Mix –

A CHILD IN FRONT OF US (*accusingly, to her mother*): I thought she said they were going to be mice.

MOTHER: Hush, dear.

ANOTHER WOMAN: She's right, you know. She did say mice.

TWO VOICES: Mice.

MANY VOICES: *Mice!*

PATTEN (*looking up, surprised*): Yes, they will indeed be very nice.

Ill-controlled titters.

PATTEN (*continuing, but nervously*): Now these two pieces of marzipan will do very well for bunny's ears, and this little blob of Pearce Duff's reconstituted cream –

SMALL BOY (*loudly and firmly*): MICE.

PATTEN (*baffled, losing hold, waving back at him insanely*): And hi to you too! So we put a little blob of Pearce D –

General shout of laughter.

PATTEN: – Duff's reconstituted cream for bunny's little tail –

Everyone in audience now weeping with mirth. Patten stops dead. Looks frantically at prompt corner, at blancmange, at the cooker, at her bra strap.

PATTEN (*heroically, above the din*): And now some whiskers for our little rabbit. . .

Her assistant collapses on to a chair, heaving, an eggwhisk dangling from her hand. Patten turns sharply, claps her hands, and the girl, tears streaming down her face, brings her some strips of angelica in a spoon. Patten's hands are shaking, drops spoon. Assistant goes back for more. Patten wordlessly scatters angelica in the general direction of the alleged rabbit, looks again at prompt corner. Band begins to play, a rumba. Traverse curtains close, leaving Patten downstage next to table bearing bowl of fruit salad. She bows deeply, like Wolfit at end of King Lear. Thunderous applause. Black out.

Royal Court Theatre
Liverpool
November 1961

On Sunday the Remembrance Day service was held on the steps of St. George's Hall. A fine drizzle, hundreds of black umbrellas. Brass band, robed civic dignitaries, the British Legion. Speeches, hymns, prayers. A gun went off somewhere by the river, in Lime Street a bus driver switched off his engine, and all was still. And then,

5

about half way through the two minutes, an elderly woman not far from where I was standing began to sing, in a clear, cultured soprano, 'For Those in Peril on the Sea'. Hundreds of astonished seagulls rose with one cry, swooped over our heads and vanished. The voice carried on, defining the silence around it. People were looking hard at their feet, but when the second gun banged and she was still singing, there seemed to be a reluctance to break the tension. And then a dribble of traffic started to come round the corner and people slowly began to disperse. A middle-aged man standing nearby waited until the end of the verse and then put his umbrella over her and took her by the arm. Absolutely nobody giggled.

Liverpool is very lively, lots going on. The trouble with the lively dates is that you wish you were here doing something different. I don't think I can *remember* doing anything different. This is week fifteen of the twenty-six week tour. Next week, the Globe Theatre Stockton-on-Tees. No, really.

Pacitto's Coffee Bar
Stockton-on-Tees
November 1961

Yes, well. Rather cheered this morning by receiving a fan letter purporting to be from MRS. ANGIOLINA TABONE, GILI'S DISPENSARY, SLEEMA, MALTA, and containing some raffle tickets for a local school playing field. If it is you really, I'd rather you didn't tell me, because it's the best thing that's happened this week.

Oh, except that I went to the pictures and saw *War-lords of Crete*, which is a must for any serious student of Hellenic mythology. Theseus falls into the sea, you remember, and beneath the waves he meets a lady a bit like Lotte Haas in a turquoise bathing costume, who tells him, 'I am Aphrodite, the Water Goddess. O, Theseus, thinkest thou because I am a goddess I do not have desires like mortal women?' A little later, Theseus goes in search of the Minotaur, a smallish kindly creature not unlike Yogi Bear. Minos, King of Crete, rides up.

THE PEOPLE: Hail, mighty Minos.

MINOS (*urgently*): Where's Theseus?

A CRETAN: He's in the labyrinth.

That's all from Stockton-on-Tees.

Rothesay
Isle of Bute
November 1961

Wish you were here. Steamer from Wemyss Bay up the Kyles of Bute and back, wonderful in the brief pale sunlight, the heather, the green sea, little white stone cottages turning pink now as the sun sinks down and I have to get the boat back to Gourock and train to Glasgow for the show.

Mrs. Mundy, my landlady, speaks almost entirely in proverbs. 'Every man's tale's guid till anither be tauld', 'He as cheats me anes, shame fa him; twice, shame fa me', and today, 'Come a' to Jock Fool's house, ye s'll get

7

bread and cheese'. I don't believe she's Scots at all. I've got into the habit of sharing digs (though not a bedroom) with the Company Manager, Bertie Parham – he's about seventy, and reminds me of Leslie Henson. He seems to regard me as his natural contemporary in the company, presumably because I'm playing a character his age, and about two and a half times my own. He's been in the business a very long time, and is very informative. Somewhere – Leeds I think it was – our landlady asked us to sign the visitors' book and then turned back the pages to show us names of the famous performers she'd had to stay in the past. I noticed that some of the signatories had added the initials 'L.D.O.' after their names, and I wondered what this stood for. 'Licentiate of Dramatic Orthodoxy' seemed unlikely, so I asked Bertie later.

'Coded information', he told me. 'Landlady's Daughter Obliges.'

Grand Theatre
Blackpool
Christmas Evening 1961

Two shows on Christmas Day is the tradition in Blackpool; and indeed it's rather nice to be working, instead of eating fragments of chicken beneath three genitally-disposed balloons in Mrs. Bishop's front room. A far cry indeed from last Christmas and the tinkling angels on your mother's table in lovely Abinger.

Nearly every house on the sea front, and in most of the streets leading to it, is a bed-and-breakfast, and, as you pass by, every window shows you the same picture – family of four eating, paper hats, balloons, holly. None of them look happy, especially Mum, presumably in consideration for whom they have shut up house and spent money on two days among total strangers.

For it is only two days, or perhaps four at most. And while it lasts, the theatres are packed, the Tower Ballroom with its Mighty Wurlitzer is in full swing, hundreds of dogs are being exercised on the snow-covered beach, and the decorated trams are crammed to the doors. But on Tuesday, the town will be deserted. Crisp packets and cigarette cartons will blow along the empty promenade, the whelk stalls and amusement arcades will be shuttered till Easter, and we at the Grand Theatre will be lucky to see two hundred souls a night.

I'm sharing digs with a man who is playing King Rat in the panto on the South Pier. On their first night, the unaccustomed heat from the stage lighting melted the packed snow on the roof, and it came pouring in through the flies. The actual heating has broken down, and audiences sit in their overcoats and gloves. The six chorus girls dance in thick woollen stockings, and my friend wears a selection of pullovers under his rat costume. I've offered to go to a matinée, but he says not to. He has the most appalling cold, and I'm getting it.

There are no such things as theatrical lodgings in Wilmslow. After a whole wet Sunday of searching, Andy and I felt we were faced with three alternatives: to commute nightly from Manchester, to take out an overdraft and stay in Prestbury, or to set fire to the theatre. In the end we went and had a drink in this pub and pleaded with the landlord, who obligingly turned his two sons out of their bedrooms for us. I've no idea where they went. Andy's room has two bicycles and a lot of unfinished model aircraft, mine has about thirty pictures of Cliff Richard. When I drew the curtains, a host of decomposing small insects fell on my head. The largest mouse in Cheshire has just gone under the wardrobe, waiting until I put the light out so that it can come out and eat this letter.

When the show was booked in here at the Rex, I don't think it can have been made clear that there is a complete set change involved. The stage staff here are employed part time, so that on matinée days they're driving buses or delivering the afternoon post. Bertie asked for volunteers from the company to go up to the flies for the change (hemp lines here, no counterweights). I couldn't, because I'm on stage at the time, but the final crew consisted of Bob Vahey, Pat Carter, the Theatre Manager and his son, and the Chef from the café next door, in his white hat.

Only two more weeks of the tour to go, then back on the dole. I haven't been able to save much out of £22.10s a week. Hey ho.

After Simple Spymen, *I appeared in* Lady Windermere's Fan *at the New Theatre, Bromley; and then was lucky enough to be included in the cast of David Rudkin's remarkable play* Afore Night Come *for the Royal Shakespeare Company's experimental season at the Arts Theatre. This meant my rehearsing as a homicidal young Worcestershire pear picker during the day, and climbing into full evening dress as Lord Augustus Lorton at Bromley in the evenings.*

Naturally when this was over nobody had the least idea how to cast me, so I joined the BBC Radio Drama Repertory Company for a happy twelve months, emerging in 1963 to get married, and to play the village idiot in Robert Bolt's Gentle Jack *for Tennent Productions. We opened in Brighton.*

Binkie and people seem pleased at the way the show is going, but I have my doubts. Robert Bolt has written a classical play in a modern idiom, which is admirable, but it seems to me that the casting of Dame Edith throws it off balance. The central figure of the argument is Mike Bryant, and the two forces pulling at him from different directions are the financial expert (John Phillips) and the Dionysus figure (Kenneth Williams). Dame Edith's part is peripheral to the scheme of things; but with her rank, billing, and £1000 worth of pink paper taffeta from Hardy Amies, people are naturally going to think the play is supposed to be about *her*, and get confused.

She's not very happy, and Kenneth has been given free accommodation at the Royal Albion to be with her and cheer her up, which he tries very conscientiously to do. I like him greatly, and much admire the way he does the very chilling speech to the audience in Act Two, addressing them first of all in modern English, then lapsing into Elizabethan speech, then mediaeval language, Anglo-Saxon and finally just brutish noises. He's a bit frightened of it, and more so now since two furious women accosted him as we were walking down North Street, complaining that they only came to the show to see him do one of his 'Carry On' performances, and that they'd had a terrible evening and it was all his fault. It did nothing for his confidence, and I have an awful feeling he may start to camp it up in self-defence.

Poor Dame Edith has had a bad attack of food poisoning on top of everything, and last night was being terribly sick in her dressing room at the half. She is, as you know, a Christian Scientist, and refused all offers of medical assistance, only asking Tony Chardet to telephone her Adviser for counsel. This Tony duly did, and was simply given a Bible reference. 'Is that all?' he asked. 'That's all,' was the reply, 'please give my warmest regards to Dame Edith.' When he returned to the dressing room and gave his message the poor lady, bent over the washbasin, wordlessly handed him a Bible and he read out the appropriate passage. Dame Edith then straightened, thanked him, sat down, finished her make up and went on stage apparently without a qualm. It makes you think.

Gentle Jack *did not draw the Town, and came off fairly quickly. I then played an overgrown Boy Scout in James Broome Lynne's* The Trigon, *again for Tennents – which got as far as the Arts Theatre, and then stopped.*

The RSC were reviving Afore Night Come *at the Aldwych, and the actor who was playing my original part was ill, or misbehaving, or something, so they asked me back to do this and other things during the 1964 London season. I ended up being in seven out of the eight plays in the season.*

The following year one of the productions, The Jew of Malta, *was to be included in the programme at Stratford-on-Avon, so Glenda Jackson, Tony Church and I moved up there for the season, opening with* Love's Labour's Lost.

Tredington
Warwickshire
April 1965

Well, the cottage is fully habitable now, and I think you'll like it. Lion is settling in remarkably well, and now regards himself very much as a country cat. I came home last night, and he was sitting, in profile, halfway up the stairs. When I looked more closely, I saw there was also a mouse, in opposite profile, sitting facing him. This was clearly a situation to be handled with delicacy. 'Lion', I said, in a low, calm voice, 'do you want to eat that mouse, or would you rather come into the kitchen with me, and I'll open a tin of Whiskas?' He thought for a moment, then turned his back on the mouse, and trotted with me into the kitchen. A triumph, I thought, of civilised behaviour over natural instinct. I had supper, watched some television, and went up to bed, turning down the counterpane to reveal the dead mouse on my pillow.

I'm enjoying *Love's Labour's Lost* because it's such a lovely play, and I like working with John Barton who is directing our scenes with wonderful scholarly tenderness, but somehow gets the play off to a terribly gloomy start with the boys. The presence of Janet Suzman and Charlie Kay in the company does a lot to compensate for leaving John Nettleton, Ken Wynne, Paul Dawkins and the other occupants of our disreputable Dressing Room 4

15

at the Aldwych. The theatre itself, however, has a completely different feel about it. The Aldwych was bursting
with energy, always being pushed and pulled about to
try and contain a repertoire and an activity that was just
that much too big for it. Stratford by contrast is cold and
institutional and space is not a problem – you could do
The Ring here, in repertoire with *Cavalcade* and *Peer
Gynt.* It's a self-contained capsule; the townspeople care
nothing for the theatre except insofar as it's part of the
tourist business that lines their pockets; they never come
to a show, and seem distinctly unfriendly to the actors.
Was it like that when you were here? Great feeling of
camaraderie *within* the company though, and I love the
care with which everything is handled in rehearsal.

*Tredington
October 1965*

When you come back next week you'll find it all very
different. Fog on Clopton Bridge, frost on the Water
Meadows, the tourists gone. The season is too long,
there's a feeling of despondency among the company, of
hopes disappointed. In March, everyone's optimistic.
They're going to get wonderful notices, the cottage is
idyllic, there's a romantic liaison just waiting to flower,
the cricket team will triumph. October comes, and the
notices haven't mentioned them, the cottage roof leaks,
the actress has gone off with somebody else and the
cricket team's lost every match.

Timon is not the success of the season, but then I
suppose it never is. Paul Scofield is breathtaking in the
second half of the play, but I think is getting a little

16

bored in the first. At one point he has to give me a jewel out of a casket. Props have given him a lovely casket with lots of very presentable jewels – all he needs to do is to put his hand in and bring out the first one he finds. If, however, he scrabbles about in the box very deeply, as he did last night, he must eventually come to a substratum of nuts and bolts, pebbles, pieces of chalk and so on. After what seemed like five minutes, he finally produced an old hardened piece of indiarubber, and handed it over with much ceremony: 'Here, my lord, a trifle of our love.' I replied, dutifully, 'With more than common thanks I will receive it'; and Paul added, 'Yes, it is nice, isn't it.'

At a matinée last week, Paul came off after one scene and said, 'Take a look at that man sitting by himself in the front row. I'm sure it's Buster Keaton.' So we all looked when we had the chance, and the likeness was indeed uncanny. After the matinée I went for a walk through the town, and called in at a pub I'd never been to before. There, sitting at a table in a corner, was, undeniably, Buster Keaton. I went up to him. 'Mr. Keaton?' I asked. 'Yes.' He seemed surprised. I said that Mr. Scofield thought he'd spotted him in the audience. 'Yes', he said, 'I was in the vicinity, and I thought I'd better see some Shakespeare.' 'Did you enjoy it?' I asked, insanely. He considered this. 'Not much', he said finally, and went back to his drink.

In 1966 I moved with the company back to the Aldwych for a couple of productions, but there seemed not to be much on offer in the way of parts for the future, so I left the RSC in the summer and began what was to be a sixteen-year-long relation-ship with the Prospect Theatre Company, then based in Cambridge. Prospect made rather a speciality of literary pieces, and they compiled a sort of biog-raphical entertainment about Boswell and Johnson. My friend Julian Glover was playing Boswell, and I was cast in the minor role of Sir John Hawkins. The actor who was supposed to be playing Johnson for some reason never materialised. I stood in for him, day after day; and then, when it became clear that he wasn't going to turn up at all, Toby Robertson, the director, asked me if I'd mind doing it.

We toured the play in repertoire, first with Anouilh's Thieves' Carnival, and then with The Tempest, in which I played Prospero.

The following year the company went out with Farquhar's The Constant Couple and an adaptation of E.M. Forster's A Room with a View.

The Theatre at Rose Hill
Cumberland
June 1967

Rather an extraordinary journey here. Engine failure meant we missed our connection at Barrow-in-Furness, but they announced that a train which should have been going just as far as Millom, a few stations up the line, would be extended to Workington, which suited us.

When we got to Millom, Richard Cottrell, John Warner and I, we seemed to be waiting rather a long time and I got out to investigate. There was no one on the platform. There was no one else on the train. There was no one driving the train, or guarding it, or in the station building, or in the road outside, or anywhere in sight. The evening sun shone. The rooks cawed in the elms. The church clock struck 6.30. A little way down the line was a signal box, and I walked to it. The signalman was there all right, having a cup of tea, and seemed surprised to see me. I explained our situation. Nobody had told him, he said, nor as far as he knew had told anyone else, that our train was supposed to go any further. The driver and guard, he assumed, had cycled home. There was, however, another crew due to arrive on the next up train, to take our train on an Outward Bound excursion to Ravenglass, leaving at 7.20. I walked back to the train, and when the new guard appeared he kindly suggested there was no real need to wait till 7.20, and if we cared to go and have a drink in the village pub, he'd come and fetch us as soon as the Outward Bound boys had been rounded up.

So we went to the pub, and that's where all the boys were, playing a fruit machine called Super Jolly Taverner. We tried to chivvy them back to the station, and they all thought Richard, who insisted on introducing us as 'strolling players', quite hilarious. We finally got them on board, and reached Whitehaven at 8.30 – thank God we didn't have a show that night. Nowhere to eat in Whitehaven at all, but as we walked up the hill, very cross, we were met in the road by a farmer's wife who asked us if we were hungry, and took us in to minced lamb, macaroni cheese, fresh strawberries, home made fruit cake and tea.

It was a surprising afternoon, but then Rose Hill has always been surprising – this beautiful toy 120-seater theatre owned by Sir Nicholas Sekers, whose typical day starts here in his silk factory at 7.30 in the morning, after which he may fly to London or Paris for lunch and a board meeting, attend the opera at Covent Garden, and fly back to Cumberland with the principal soprano in time to appear at a party he's giving here after the show. While secretaries and attendants keel over with exhaustion, he bounds around from one pursuit to another, crying 'It will be superb!'

I love the place, and him.

Sleeping Car from Newcastle
August 1967

A good week at my favourite touring theatre, the Newcastle Theatre Royal, was somewhat marred by the most appalling digs. Fiona Walker, Hazel Coppen, Neil Stacy and I were all together, and agreed that forty-five shillings a night without breakfast for a filthy room with damp sheets and continual rudeness from the landlady was not to be borne. We had to stick it out for the week, though, because there was absolutely nowhere else, but before we left we put into operation a device from my father's touring days.

Hazel went out early to buy a pair of kippers and a screwdriver, and then while Fiona held the landlady in the kitchen in argument about the bill, Neil and I went into the front parlour, unscrewed the back of the Rexine sofa, inserted the kippers and screwed it together again. The only sadness is, of course, that we shall not be around in a week's time to savour the mature effect.

All this touring was fine, and very enjoyable, but it wasn't paying many bills. I decided I had to redress the balance with some television, and I see to my astonishment that I actually did seven television plays (none of them even vaguely memorable), and a film, Twisted Nerve, *that year.*

Then Val May, running the Bristol Old Vic Company, invited me down for James Saunders' adaptation of Iris Murdoch's The Italian Girl. *I spent a lot of my childhood in Bristol, and I loved the city's Georgian Theatre Royal, and still do.*

Enclosed is the advance publicity for the play when we transfer to the West End. I hadn't quite realised we were out to catch the Tired Business Man. When the poster comes out it'll probably be shaped like a pair of knickers. Jane Wenham had rather seen her role as the nucleus of a complex domestic intrigue, and is a little cross at being pictured as a sort of Windmill Girl. I've suggested to the Publicity Agent that we re-title it 'Huis Never Clos'.

I took the car into a Car Wash yesterday, and as I sat there with the soapy water running down the windscreen and those woolly Maurice Sendak creatures boffing away on the roof the man in front of me who'd had his Wash got out of his car and leered grotesquely at me, rolling his eyes wildly, flapping his hands and cackling loudly. He was soberly dressed, and his behaviour was very, very surprising. As my windscreen cleared, he suddenly stopped what he was doing, turned bright crimson and put a hand over his eyes. I got out. 'Look, I'm most frightfully sorry,' he said. 'Assing around like that. I couldn't see you properly. I thought you were my dentist.'

How are you in Toronto? Is it still very cold? I was home for the weekend, and got your message wanting a report on the garden.

23

The Garden. Ah, well now. Umm. Yes. *Yes.* Right you are. Well, here goes then. RIGHT. From the beginning. First things first. My general impression is that there are more leaves than flowers. That's about the size of it. More leaves than flowers. Just so. Quite a lot more, in fact. The next thing that strikes the intelligent observer is that what flowers there are, are to be found on the left, as you look out of the window. None on the right. No. What *are* these flowers, you will wish to ask? Well, they are mostly those pink ones, you know, several to a stem, also available in blue. And white too. Oh, and purple. Or are those different? Anyway, there are about ten in all.

Now I don't want to stick my neck out here, but I believe I may be right in saying there are some daffodils on the same side of the garden, and one thing I'm pretty sure of is that there were a lot more of them at this time last year. At the end of the garden we seem to have a lot of tall green stuff with small yellow bits on top. A considerable amount. Probably more than anyone else in the road.

Well, that's about it. Yes, I believe that just about wraps it up. Anything else you want to know about the garden, you know you have only to ask.

The Italian Girl *ran a happy six months in London, and I then went to Manchester for Granada's Underworld serial* Big Breadwinner Hog, *which caused something of a stir in the more excitable daily newspapers. After that I rejoined Prospect, now grown in scope and stature and presenting Ian McKellen in the two roles of Richard II and Marlowe's Edward II.*

Edinburgh Festival
August 1969

Well, it seems we're by way of being the hit of the Festival. Not just *Richard*, whose reputation has gone before it, but the Marlowe as well – Ian is magnificent in both, of course, but again we sort of know about the Richard; his Edward is a powerful surprise. Toby's done it very well – absolutely the right play for him, all furious speed and energy and no boring character details, and we've had a splendid boost from a certain Councillor Kidd, who has discovered that two men are to be seen kissing on the stage in the Assembly Hall of the Church of Scotland, and is publicly apoplectic.

Never mind the danger to the morals of the Edinburgh Burghers; the danger offered to the members of the Prospect Theatre Company fighting half-a-dozen fierce battles with heavy broadswords on a raked polished brass disc in flashing blue light, wearing masks, touches us more nearly I'm afraid. Only flesh wounds so far.

Not much time to get to anything except a few morning concerts, and a couple of late night fringe shows. Entertainment is quite lavish, but it's the usual thing, they tend to invite the same six of us to everything: and the rest of the company, who could well do with a free meal and a glass of wine, get left out. We decided to protest gently about this, and now we don't get nearly so many invitations.

It's a heady atmosphere, though. The hot summer nights, climbing in the quiet small hours up the Mound, with the moon shining on the Castle and the great gaunt gothic shape of the Assembly Hall towering above you, and feeling in a satisfied alcoholic way that, for a change, you're there for a purpose.

Bratislava
Czechoslovakia
October 1969

The reception last night after *Richard II* at the Nova Scena Theatre was extraordinary. We had assumed we were simply doing what the British Council requires, sharing a piece of our culture with the Eastern Europeans, but to the Bratislavans the story was the story of the Russian invasion. Ian therefore was Dubcek, and as Bolingbroke I therefore became the disgraceful Husek. At the final curtain they wept and shouted and threw flowers, and wouldn't let Ian go. It was I suppose the first time since the invasion that they had been given such an opportunity communally to release their feelings, and it was very humbling to see what we had done, and how little we had meant to do it.

The authorities were not so sure of our innocence. Our Press Conference on the morrow was summarily cancelled. Our hotel was changed (and Terry Wilton found a 'bug' at the back of his radio, but thought it had been there for some time.) We were not allowed out except under escort. *Before* the first performance, some of the company had experienced trouble of another sort. Jane Robertson, wearing one of those Dr. Zhivago coats

27

with fur hat and muff, had stones thrown at her in the street for looking Russian; and Paul Hardwick, with his Brezhnev eyebrows and KGB-style suit, was threatened in a bar. To make matters worse, he reasoned with his assailants in very good German, which unfortunately is the language the Russians use in Czechoslovakia to show they're not Russian. They took him round to the back of the bar, and would have given him a very serious time had he not just then found a copy of his small-pox certificate, in English, in his pocket. Then, of course, there were apologies, and kisses, and slivovitz, and one way and another it was a shaky John of Gaunt who took the stage that evening.

We met a musician, whose husband knew Toby Robertson and now lived in the UK. They had both been members of the Czech Radio Orchestra, and she had been on leave in the last stages of pregnancy when news broke of the imminent Russian invasion. Her husband was away, with the orchestra, on a European tour. She telegraphed him in London with instructions to miss the plane back, apply for political asylum, and that she would somehow join him as soon as the birth allowed. She never managed it. The terrible irony of her seeing us off at Bratislava Airport, knowing that her husband, whom she would never see again, and who would never see his child, theoretically could meet *us* three and a half hours later at Heathrow, was unbearable.

We played Richard *and* Edward *for a season at the Mermaid Theatre, televised them both, made a record of* Edward, *toured them round a bit, and finally came back to London for a triumphant run at the Piccadilly. Then I joined Diana Rigg and Keith Michell in the cast of* Abelard and Héloise *by Ronald Millar.*

Grand Theatre
Leeds
May 1970

Arrived at the theatre today to see all posters covered with flybill 'Diana and Keith Reveal All' – the work of the Theatre Manager, who is delighted with himself. So we shall have another week of nobody listening to a word anyone says until the 'nude scene' has come and gone, by which time of course my part's nearly over.

There was a Press Conference this morning in the Circle Bar, and the journalists swarmed round Diana and Keith, while Elspeth March, John Warner and I sat and had coffee undisturbed. One reporter, rather short and quite inexperienced, couldn't get a look in at either of our stars, and wandered disconsolately over to our table. He asked us if we were in the play, and we assured him we were. He couldn't think of anything to ask us, so not to waste time I interviewed him; where was he born and educated, what made him take up journalism, did he follow football and so on. It was quite a good interview, though I say it myself, and I've sent it to his Editor.

1970 was a busy year. I had negotiated an early release from Abelard and Héloise *to go and do the Dr Johnson play again for Prospect at the Edinburgh Festival, after which it was back to London for Harold Pinter's production of James Joyce's* Exiles *at the Mermaid. The Sunday morning after we finished that, I flew to Madrid to start work on the Monday on the film* Nicholas and Alexandra.

When I got to Heathrow, someone from the film company came up to me with a large green suitcase and asked if I'd mind taking it out to Madrid with me – it was wardrobe stuff, he said. His credentials were OK, he paid the excess baggage and showed some sort of docket at the check-in; the case had already been examined, apparently, and so it went through with my own.

It occurred to me during the flight that I hadn't looked at the case very closely, and I hoped it was properly labelled because otherwise I couldn't be absolutely certain I'd recognise it again.

No, if it had ever had a company label, it must have come off. There were about ten possibles going round the baggage carousel; most of these were duly claimed, and the choice was gradually whittled down to two. I peered closely at both – one of them was labelled 'Garcia' and the other 'Jackson', but no addresses. By this time I was the only person left at the carousel, and the Guardia Civil had been watching me with growing interest. I opted finally for Jackson, and was preparing to sail through the green channel when I was stopped by a Customs official and taken into a small office.

'Is this your case, señor?'

'I think so.'

'You think so. Is your name Jackson?'

'No.'

'Passport please. Why have you taken Señor Jackson's case?'

I explained.

'A Russian film? Here in Madrid? What is in this case?'

'Well – clothes, I suppose. They said it was for Wardrobe. Costumes.'

With some difficulty, the officer lifted the heavy case on to his desk. He undid it, and lifted the lid a fraction. Then he shut it again very quickly. Was I wrong, or did I catch the glimmerings of a smile?

'You have no idea', he asked again slowly, 'exactly what is in this case?'

I shook my head.

'Look', he said, and opened it fully. What the case contained was, indisputably, the Crown Jewels. Orb, sceptre, a few coronets and tiaras, a vast amount of flamboyant jewellery. I was aware that no Russian State Occasion was to be passed over in this film, and the intention clearly was to show that the Romanoffs were never knowingly underdressed.

The Customs officer fell about, and let me go. So if you're ever tempted to steal any genuine crown jewels, this is the way to go about it.

The film unit is cosmopolitan. Sparks are Spanish of course, Camera, Sound and Props British, Construction Italian for some reason, the First Assistant Spanish, the Second American. Make-up British, with Turkish assistant. Second Unit Director French. My dresser is called Pablo. He is very beautiful and wears pastel-coloured angora pullovers, and if he gets any dirt on them he *cries*. Franklin J. Schaffner, the Director (he did 'Patten') is tall and grey and handsome in a superb three-

33

piece suit with a Phi Beta Kappa fob on his watch-chain. I like him, and he was very kind to me when I kept fluffing on my first day.

The writers come and go with the speed of light, mostly because Sam Spiegel changes such a lot of what they've done. Janet Suzman as Alexandra, hysterical over the condition of the haemophilic infant Tsarevitch, had a line: 'My baby's dying, there's no medicine – Christ Jesus!' This was altered to: 'My baby's dying – there's no medicine. Good heavens!' In the early part of the script, Sam's demands for clarification of identity have led to a lot of 'Hello Trotsky, meet Lenin, where's Stalin, have you seen Martov' kind of thing. But we have two Advisers – one (Historical), the legendary Baroness Myra Budberg: once Gorki's mistress, then H. G. Wells's, knew Rasputin and in fact was at Prince Youssoupov's party when the Prince and his companions were killing the man, downstairs. Apparently she spent the time thinking what a bad host Youssoupov was being, popping in nervously to swig some champagne before disappearing again, presumably to chain up his recalcitrant victim and drop him through the ice. Maurice Denham and I took her out to supper and listened enthralled to all this while she ate three lobsters, cracking them open energetically and spattering the other diners with pieces of shell. I think she had a good evening.

The other Adviser (Text) is favourite David Giles. He doesn't know, he says, quite what he's being paid for, but is careful to wear an expression of judgment and forethought in case anyone should approach him for an opinion on anything. He's a refreshingly fixed point in this sometimes rather dotty world of international movies, and we sit on the caravan steps talking about Mrs. Mackay's Boarding House in Daisy Avenue, Manchester.

Michael Jayston (Nicholas) has decided to quarrel with Sam Spiegel, and keeps thinking up imaginative ways to annoy him. Spiegel hates dogs, and Michael does a tremendously good canine impression. There is a ventilation duct running down the wall of the make-up room, which continues down into Sam Spiegel's office below. Michael's trick is to go into Make-up, bark through a grille in the ventilation duct, and then run out to the top of the stairs to hear Sam shouting that there is a dog somewhere in his office, and will someone come at once and get it out. I question the political wisdom of this exercise, but it is huge fun.

They're letting us home for Christmas after all. I hope to get on the 4.15 Iberia flight on Christmas Eve.

Hotel Sanvy
Madrid
February 1971

If this letter reads like Jennifer's Diary, you'll have to excuse me, but it does seem as though every British actor Sam Spiegel has ever heard of has got a part somewhere in this film. Various distinguished people have been coming over for the political scenes, wearing more or less identical Tsarist uniforms, moustaches, beards and pince-nez. I was just starting my lunch in the otherwise empty canteen when one such person came in, his beard slightly unstuck and a lot of cigarette ash down the front of his uniform.

'Hello, Timothy,' he said. Now, not many people have called me Timothy since the headmistress of my primary school, and then only when she was cross; so I concluded this was an actor who didn't know me very well. A two-day broadcast together perhaps, or maybe a special week at Worthing. I said it was nice to see him, and asked if he had just arrived. Yesterday, he said. And would he be here long? About eight days. Oh good, I said; well, think you'll like the Unit, and I hope you have a good time; have you got somewhere nice to stay? Oh yes, he said. So I thought, well, I've done that, I've been welcoming, and my mackerel's getting cold; so I said, 'See you around, then,' and sat down to eat my lunch. Something about the look of his back, as he walked away towards Mr. Spiegel's regular table, made my blood suddenly run cold. For the next week, whenever I met him, I tried to get as many 'Sir Laurence's into a sentence as it could syntactically bear.

Michael Redgrave is here too, and he and Harry Andrews took Janet and me to Alcala de Henares (Cervantes' birthplace), and gave us tea and scones. It felt a bit like a half-term treat with a couple of maiden aunts, and was very pleasurable.

The thing I'll probably remember most about this picture is having had the privilege of working with Jack Hawkins, on what I think must have been his last movie. His constant courage and unwavering commitment, battling to speak through a hole in his throat, was phenomenal. We took him and his wife Pat to a tabla one night to see some flamenco, and the principal dancer stopped between numbers and called, 'Welcome to Spain Mr. Hack Awkins', and invited him up to dance, which he did. And then, while Pat sat at our table screwing up her eyes in pain at the effort it must be costing him, Jack entertained the audience with a very funny story, delivered quite clearly, and got all his laughs.

You mustn't think all my time is spent gallivanting with the great. I've had a few days off, and try to divide my time properly. So many hours with Hugo's *Spanish in Three Months*, so many hours at the Prado; so many hours must I contemplate, so many hours must I sport myself . . .

Talking about sport, I saw a bull fight last week. Very clever Matador, but I still find it loathsome. Mustn't say so though.

Several very interesting jobs in 1971.

Charles Marowitz, who was running the Open Space Theatre with which I had become connected, had to go into hospital for a minor operation. While he was convalescing, someone brought him a collection of Oscar Wilde's essays. Wilde might seem of all possible authors the least likely to appeal to Marowitz, a black-sweatered, iconoclastic New Yorker; but he was so struck with one particular essay, 'The Critic as Artist', that he immediately set about adapting it as a short two-handed play, and we did it at the Open Space.

I also had the good fortune to be cast by Mike Apted in Alun Owen's play Joy *for BBC TV.*

Then Toby Robertson invited me to do Lear *for Prospect, opening as was customary at the Edinburgh Festival and then touring in company with* Love's Labour's Lost.

Edinburgh Festival
1971

Well, here we are again, my fourth Edinburgh Festival in five years, and my first time for being bang in the middle of it – King Lear, eh, at thirty-seven, ridiculous. No, not quite ridiculous; I think the energy you have when you're younger is important, not just technically, but because I believe Lear is still quite an energetic man at the beginning. I know we don't quite agree on this, but I'm positive Shakespeare intends him to be culpable, to have committed the worst Shakespearean sin in the book, that of arbitrarily discarding the responsibilities of power, and thereby destroying order. If he's already too weak for office, his abdication is reasonable, and, all right, you can sympathise with him, but you should be furious with him as well.

I like the production a lot – very stark, a bare stage, the costumes all of the same material, colour and design, so no prejudgments to be made about any of the charac- ters. Lighting pretty well constant, snatches only of music; it's all down to the actors and to the text. Well, see what you think.

The first night seemed to go all right, and we had a bit of a party, but when I finally got to bed, I dreamed that the whole of the next morning's edition of the Daily Telegraph was devoted to a bad notice for my Lear. It started with the headlines on the front page, ran through the home news, the foreign news, sport, the weather forecast, even the crossword. There was one line in the review that I remembered word for word when I woke up: 'Worst of all, he allows a decimal tear to dew the crest of his sugary cheek, at the point of the famed "head-lugg'd bear" speech.'

Now, as you know, the 'head-lugg'd bear' speech is a real speech, only it happens to occur in a scene when Lear is not even on stage. I knew this, even in my dream, and thought it was terribly unfair. Carrying the paper, I went to see my mother, who for the purposes of the dream was living in a flooded basement a few streets away. She was wearing a black shawl over her head, and was rocking and keening like some bereaved crone out of Sean O' Casey. The flood water came up above her ankles, and pieces of the Daily Telegraph were floating about in it, so I knew she'd seen the notice. I started to complain of the injustice, but she carefully avoided my eye and went on rocking – it was clear that she actually agreed with the reviewer. I was desperate. 'But mother,' I pleaded, 'the head-lugg'd bear speech is Albany's speech to Goneril, I'm not even *on* . . .'

She looked up at me with a deep sadness and compassion. 'Darling,' she said. 'People run out of acting, just as I sometimes run out of butter.'

When I woke up, at about 7.30, I went straight out and bought the Daily Telegraph. It certainly wasn't a rave, but it wasn't as bad as all that.

Pru had brought our five-year-old son Sam up to Scotland to see King Lear – *at his own suggestion I think – and he became so intoxicated with the atmosphere of the Edinburgh Festival that when his mother had to return to London she left him in my care, and that of the* Lear *company, for a few days. Everyone in the cast took a turn at escorting him round the various events.*

University Hostel
The Mound
Edinburgh
September 1971

Sam had a pretty good time I think. I took him to the
Tattoo at the Castle. The pipers played a march, and he
looked solemn and clapped his little hands vigorously.
'Did you like that?' I asked. 'No,' he said, 'but it must be
so difficult.'

I've taken your Notes to heart, and introduced them
into the performance stealthily, one by one. People are
generally enthusiastic, in spite of the fact that it's a pretty
gruelling experience for all, in that baking hot auditorium with no air-conditioning and megawatts of lighting
only a few feet from their heads. For us, seven performances a week in these conditions feels like a lot. I've
been prescribed salt pills, just as if we were in India. The
house is always full, and business is very good for the
Tour, and Australia is now definite.

The company were entertained to lunch by NATO at
Leith, on board various ships. You could choose. Most
people went for the exciting technology of the US
aircraft carrier – wily old Trevor Martin and I, remem-
bering that the US Navy is Dry, opted for the Dutch
frigate, and had a very jolly time.

The real stars of this Festival are the Bulandra Theatre
Company of Rumania. They are brilliant, as well as being

42

wonderful people; and so seem all their compatriot painters, sculptors, dancers and musicians brought over this year by Ricky de Marco. A whole lot of them came to a matinée, we had a riotous tea in Prince's Street among a lot of Morningside ladies in hats, and we were each of us individually invited to Bucharest. By the Rumanians, I mean, not the Morningside ladies.

Last night, Michael Griffiths put his head round the door while I was making up and asked: 'What did the short-sighted ornithologist say when he found himself on Easter Island?'

'I don't know, Michael, what?'

'Owl – owl? OWL? Ohhhh – you are MEN, of STONES . . . '

King Lear *and* Love's Labour's Lost *went to Australia – I took the family – then toured the UK, and finished up with a fortnight at the Aldwych. I played Sir William Gower in a musical version of* Trelawny of the Wells *to open Bristol's newly refurbished Royal; and a little later, Falstaff in both parts of* Henry IV *at the same theatre.*

There was also a BBC TV series about eminent Edwardians, in which I played the outrageous swindler Horatio Bottomley, Member of Parliament for Hackney and editor of John Bull Magazine. He breakfasted, every day of his working life, on kippers and Champagne. Throughout rehearsals I followed his example, for purposes of research, and I can't recommend it too highly.

And then to Paris, for the film The Day of the Jackal.

Paris
September 1972

Anton Rogers and I have been put into a very smart Dutch-operated hotel, which we must get out of as soon as possible and find somewhere Parisian and not nearly so expensive. In my bedroom there is a drinks dispenser with a keyboard, like a piano. If you want a whisky, with soda and ice, you play a sort of triad in G major, and the three elements come together in a glass. A chord of D 7th gets you vodka, tonic, ice and a slice of lemon. It's a wonderful game, and Anton and I sit on the end of my bed saying, 'do you know this one – I'll play it to you', and of course while you're composing, a colossal bill is being run up on a computer somewhere; we can't stand it for long.

A very nice easy atmosphere at the studios, which are just across the Bois de Boulogne. You arrive about nine thirty, and don't do much before lunch, which is a social occasion. Then you get down to it, and by eight o'clock you've put really quite a lot in the can. Fred Zinneman is of course splendid, and the French actors charming. I'm a bit worried about playing a French official who is really just one of a group of officials played by genuine Frenchmen, and on my arrival, put this to Fred. 'Smoke a Gauloise, and shrug your shoulders a lot', was his advice, which I laughed off, naturally. I went away and practised varying degrees of a French accent, studied my French

45

colleagues' body language, their speech patterns, moustaches and Mediterranean tans. In the end, I hit on the idea of smoking a Gauloise, and cunningly introduced a clever shrug of the shoulders, which I thought very French.

In my earlier days, in Rep., I'd done quite a lot of directing, and enjoyed it. However, it is both practically and economically difficult for a director to set aside the time he or she needs to plan a production in advance, while at the same time pursuing an acting career and consequently wanting to move on to the next job as quickly as possible.

Nevertheless, I'd been thinking it was time I did a bit more of it, and when the offer came from the management of the Forum Theatre, Billingham, to put together a company and run it for a season, choosing my own plays, I accepted in a spirit of adventure.

Billingham Forum
Teesside
February 1973

This place is quite unlike any in which I have ever worked. To start with, the town. Sandwiched between Stockton and Middlesbrough, it became the centre for ICI's extensive chemical industry, and developed, rather uneasily, into a self-contained Borough. Vast chemical works, housing estates for the employees, and a small pedestrian area with shops, one hotel, one church, a Technical College, a Chinese restaurant – and the Billingham Forum.

The Forum is a huge social complex comprising a swimming pool, an ice rink, squash and badminton courts, boxing and wrestling rings, saunas, a restaurant, bars, and a very good theatre. When you come in through the front entrance, you have a choice. You can turn left up carpeted stairs between attractively-papered walls past a pleasantly-lit cocktail bar with reproduction furniture and little nuts in the ashtrays, to where a smiling girl in a black dress will show you to a comfortable seat in the auditorium. Or you can turn right, in which case linoleumed steps will bring you to a somewhat larger bar, with formica table tops, fruit machines, a dart board and a juke box. Beyond this, the sports facilities beckon.

Well, it's not hard to guess which way ninety-eight per cent of the inhabitants choose to go. The identifiable

48

theatre audiences hitherto have driven over from Durham, Hartlepool or Bishop Auckland, whenever there was a touring show with a star who took their fancy. But a season here of home-produced plays, such as I'm attempting, is not a new idea – George Roman did it back when the theatre first opened – and economically, it's not all that much of a risk; the considerable rates that ICI pay the Borough fund its leisure services very generously, including the theatre. The overheads are all looked after, the workshops are excellent, the Production Manager and a couple of full-time skilled carpenters are paid for by the Borough.

The thing is, though, to get people somehow to change their habits, and realise that they're not going to be struck dead if they feel they'd like to have a swim *and* see a play.

Certain potent forces stand in the way, apart from that terrible decision to be made at the front door. The Commissionaire, with fearsome visage and rows of medal ribbons some of which must date back to the Crimea, scares the living daylights out of most potential patrons, particularly the young ones, whom he actually tells to go away. The nice couple who run the garage told me they've often thought of coming, but can't really afford to close early so that he can go home and put on a suit and she can go into Stockton to get her hair done. The students at the Technical College think it's for the nobs. The shopkeepers think it's just for the visitors. The people who go over to the theatre in Darlington believe we're Amateurs.

So it was not easy to put on a brave face to meet my Company when they arrived wonderingly at Billingham's graffiti-sprayed railway halt on Monday. Good heavens, I thought, what am I doing to these people, Julian Glover,

Keith Drinkel, Elizabeth Counsell, Peter Postlethwaite, Roland Curram, Carol Gillies, taking them away from their families and friends to spend weeks upon weeks in this forbidding place, and with no guarantee that anyone at all is going to come and see them. And so *many* of them; Les Jobson, the Theatre Manager, has insisted that we only do large-cast plays, he has the budget for it, in fact I've worked out that we can support a theatre-in-education team as well. What are they all going to do, and where are they all going to *live?* Where are *you* going to live, when you come up to direct *The Double Dealer?* I mean. With *me*, I hope, but I haven't found a house yet, it's very difficult. At present, I'm in a student hostel; a one-foot-nine-inch bed with nylon sheets, out of which I fall, hourly. A janitor with a savage bull-terrier called Butch roams the corridors at night making sure there's no hanky-panky.

Chance'd be a fine thing.

The Billingham Arms
April 1973

Everyone seems to have been delighted with *The Double Dealer*, and I shall remember Roly and Carol's Poetry Scene as one of the most perfectly played pieces of comedy ever. *The National Health* is shaping well, I think, and booking too, which is hugely encouraging. Perhaps we really are getting somewhere. The company have been terrific; apart from working their socks off with T.I.E., with lunchtime and late-night shows, and even one attempt at street theatre, they've made friends generally in the town, and people stop us now in the shopping precinct to ask how the show's going. It may not be too long before they feel able to make the leap to come and see for themselves.

So morale is good, and getting better now the weather's warmer. The sea's not far away, and there is some lovely country once you get beyond all those gargantuan ICI pipes running along both sides of the road. (I had a terrible dream the other night about that long road, which is called Belassis Avenue, and in my dream I contracted a disease called belassis, which is essentially a stasis of the belly. It swelled and swelled, and turned a rich purple; ah, they said, you've been driving down Belassis Avenue, haven't you – did you have the window open? There's nothing we can do, they said, if you've really got belassis.)

I'm afraid Benn Levy's new play isn't going to work out. As you know, he terribly wants a grand female star, and doesn't understand about Billingham and that we'd never get the sort of person he's thinking of with no guarantee of a transfer. Time is running out anyway, so we're going to have to drop it. Les wants a Shaw, and I'm keen to do *Major Barbara*. I'm going to ask Lynn Farleigh, get someone else to direct it, and perhaps supply and fit my own Undershaft.

They seem to want me for the *Edward VII* telly, which is rather exciting. That means I'll have to put a locum in for the second season here, having chosen the programme, and they understand that and have been very nice about it.

Edward VII took up all my time for about ten months, with two weeks' rehearsal and a week in the studio for each episode (a full week because the sets were so large they couldn't all fit in at the same time), and an additional eight weeks on film all around the country. Such a schedule would be laughed at today, but the results justified the time and care.

Next summer I went to Chichester to play Shpigelsky in A Month in the Country *for Toby, and then to the Gardner Centre in Brighton to assist John David in his season there; playing Macbeth, George in* Jumpers *and directing Pinter's* The Homecoming.

A bit more television, notably Malcolm Bradbury's The After Dinner Game, *and a silly film,* Soft Beds – Hard Battles *with Peter Sellers, and then in 1975 I played Judge Brack in Trevor Nunn's production of* Hedda Gabler, *with Glenda Jackson as the eponymous manuscript-burner. We went on a World Tour.*

Princess Theatre
Melbourne
February 1975

Arrived this morning drunk with jet-lag and exhausted from our 24-hour stopover in Singapore. Well. Rent-an-Ambience. Instant Oriental Experience. Scarcely have you apologised for tripping over a limbless beggar on the pavement, when your attention is caught by an elegant lady in a samfoo with a parasol and a dainty basket, bargaining for star-fruit. And then along comes a rickshaw, its passenger a 120-year old Indian in pristine white robes, his beard reaching to his knees. Laundry hangs in festoons from poles overhead. Most people seem to be children. Some of them really do come up and say you want to meet my sister she plenty good jig jig.

The shops are wonderful, dark behind green canvas flaps; their owners sitting on the ground spinning, measuring meal, buying gold. The harbour crammed, cheek by jowl, with every kind of boat; British warships, Arab dhows, Chinese junks, Malayan tramp steamers, fishing boats, luxury yachts. Men looking like Peter Lorre giving terse commands to accomplices and then roaring off in motor launches, threading their way miraculously under the bows of the shipping.

Raffles' Hotel rather forlorn now. Didn't stay to eat there – instead had a wonderful piecemeal picnic from the various mobile hot food stalls that move into the central Car Park at dusk; and took a tri-shaw at midnight to Bugis Street, the established venue for open-air drag parties. The first person I met (in male attire) was one of the Elstree cameramen. He told me that just a moment ago he had come upon the editor of a popular British weekly magazine, and indicated a table at which were sitting three ladies whom I might have taken to be Maxine Audley, Vittoria de los Angeles and Barbara Cartland. I don't know which one of them was the Editor, but it does show you're not safe with your little secret even in Singapore.

And now it's lovely to be back in Australia. The hotel is called the Chateau Commodore, and it tries valiantly to live up to the dual responsibilities of its name. Norman Baronial and 18th Century Maritime are an unusual combination of styles, and polished binnacles and schooners in glass cases do not happily complement the claymores, targes and stags' heads in the residents' lounge, any more than the false open stone fireplace in the front hall looks quite right between two brass portholes. The bedrooms have opted out of the contest, and are sort of Hendon Neo-Jacobean.

Edward VII is going out here currently on Channel 7, and under its original title instead of, as in the USA, *Edward the King*. (As opposed to Edward the Quantity Surveyor, or Edward the Chiropodist. The Americans originally wanted to call it *The Royal Victorians*, till I pointed out that the king was more by way of being a Royal Edwardian. I suggested *Bert and Vicky and Ted and Alex*, but they didn't go for it.) Anyway, here it's apparently scoring 28 points against the Ernie Sigley Show, which I'm told is very satisfactory.

I was on a chat show for Channel 7 the other night, hosted by a lady who was grounded two years ago for bad language, and is back now but very nervous. Doesn't listen to a word anyone says, and keeps looking at the monitor. Plucks continuously at her armpits saying how hot the studio is. The show lasts about three hours, and the audience are given beer and the racing to watch on another channel in case they get bored, which they do, very early on. I talked for about 18 seconds, then there was 25 minutes of sports footage, after which I had another quick burst; there were a lot of commercials, and then a pop group, and finally a serious man with bare knees and a whistle hung round his neck came on, and spoke about fire risks in the Dandenongs. They only had me because they couldn't get Glenda. Someone must have warned her.

Elizabethan Theatre
Newtown
Sydney
1 March 1975

The Sydney Scene is rather fierce with the late nights, but the extraordinary thing is you never feel tired here. People are being smashing to us, and all the friends from last time send love to you and the boys.

This is a big Edwardian (not Elizabethan) theatre a little way out of the centre of the City; do you remember we came here to see the last performance of the Australian Ballet Season, *Cinderella*, with Helpmann and Ashton giving their Ugly Sisters for the very last time? The place is to be demolished soon apparently, and they've taken up all the carpets. It's like a huge tropical railway station to play in, and you have to yell above the noise of the trains and the street traffic and the fidgeting of people stuck to their seats in the intolerable heat. There's no air conditioning, so they leave the lantern in the roof open and those huge flying black beetles come in, and swoop down on to the stage. They have a particular fondness for Glenda's wig, and want to nest in it – she's wonderful, never bats an eyelid, but the effect is a bit Charles Addams.

Kate Fitzpatrick has fallen heavily for Trevor, and at a party the other night kept sitting in front of him looking uncharacteristically soulful. I asked her what she thought she was doing, and she said she was playing it Jewish and Darkly Intellectual, but she didn't appear to me to be getting anywhere. She is, incidentally, brilliant in *Ride Across Lake Constance* at the Nimrod's very good new premises. Hugh Hunt's *Peer Gynt* at the Opera House worthy and old-fashioned, but masterly compared with the Melbourne Theatre Company's *Double Dealer*, under an English director who had clearly decided that no one in the audience would understand the words and therefore had introduced so much fan-tapping, handkerchief-waving, tinkling laughter and skipping about, that of course nobody did.

Quotes of the week:

(1) 'Will you be bringing a man or a gentleman?' – John Tasker with a hangover, asking me to dinner.

(2) 'Just put me anywhere at all – two in the sixth or seventh row stalls, on the aisle, will be just dandy' – Bette Davis asking Glenda for seats for the first night, which has been booked out since January.

(3) 'Final recognition of Adelaide-born Keith Michell's talents as UK's top actor-manager came with his appointment last year as director of the Chester Festival. His production of Ibsen's *A Month in the Country* was the great success of the English Theatrical Season' – TV Week.

Royal Hawaiian Hotel
Honolulu
April 1975

Well, while you're in Nottingham, I'm sitting under the stars on Waikiki Beach, sipping an exotic drink in the torchlight and talking romantically to Connie Chapman about Douglas Morris and the kind of salaries he pays at the Bristol Old Vic.

We have a two day break here, because in crossing the date-line from west to east we get two Sundays in a row. Very pleasant, but it would be nice to get out of Honolulu and see more Polynesians and fewer fat American ladies with those triangular white beaks on their noses.

Our two sons Sam and Joe, in the care of their half-sister Juliet, came out to join me in the United States, for two weeks in California and two in Washington, DC. In Hollywood we were put into a small self-catering hotel with a pool, which was fine. And we hired a car. But Juliet, at 18, couldn't quite reconcile the Hollywood of myth with the Hollywood of tawdry reality.

Huntington Hartford Theater
Hollywood, California
April 1975

The first thing to hit us here was the Oscar Ceremonies. You probably read about the furore – during the presentations, Bob Hope and Frank Sinatra made an announcement purporting to come from the Board of the Academy, castigating one of the winners for improper conduct. The award in question was for a documentary on Vietnam, and during his acceptance speech the director had read out a telegram from a Vietcong General, corroborating the facts shown in the film and expressing his approval. Maybe it was pretty tactless, but the point is that Hope and Sinatra had cooked up the reprimand between them and delivered it as though coming from the Academy Board, whom they hadn't even approached. Most people here don't seem to think that mattered, though.

Hollywood, as a district, is very odd. Of course it's quite a way from Los Angeles itself, and until you get out in the other direction to the Gracious Homes of Beverly Hills, all you have are a few streets of sleazy massage parlours, cheap tourist shops and a Howard Johnson's. 'Hollywood and Vine' is just an intersection of two such dismal thoroughfares; anything that happened here happened a long time ago, and the brass stars let into the sidewalk, to commemorate the great, feel like their tombstones. But this is where we're going to live, Juliet and me and the boys, for the next two weeks, and we shall make the best of it.

The first night party was attended by Greer Garson, Valentina Cortese, George Segal, Francis Ford Coppola and James Stewart, not that they spoke to anyone except Glenda. But I met a terribly nice couple who, blow me, invited our kids off to Disneyland tomorrow – I can't go as we have a rehearsal – and asked me to join them for supper after the show. They have a boy about Sam's age, and could not possibly have been more welcoming.

Hedda is a huge hit. I got Juliet in by graft the other night, and just as she'd gone inside I was offered $100 by a man for a seat. Too late to call her back, give him the ticket, let her see the show in Washington on a $20 standby and make eighty on the deal, damn.

Sheraton Hotel
Washington, DC
May 1975

I feel I should now give you a detailed account of how we lost Joe. Both the boys were very sleepy on the flight, and Juliet was suffering with tonsillitis. We arrived here at Dulles Airport, with me keeping an eye on Sam, and Juliet on Joe, who suddenly got very lively and asked me for money to go and buy some sweets. The company's bus then arrived, and I called Joe, and we all got on the bus. I thought. Juliet lay on the back seat with a rug over herself and, I supposed, Joe. So it wasn't until we reached the Sheraton, twenty miles away, that his absence was discovered.

I found the hotel manager's wife, who burst into tears at the news, and together we rang Airport Security, the Pan Am desk, the Duty Manager, everyone we could think of, without eliciting any news of Joe's where-abouts; and finally she offered to drive me back to the Airport.

She was in a terrible state, and kept taking her hands off the wheel to find her tissues. 'Oh that poor little BOY', she kept sobbing, the car weaving across the freeway as she blew her nose. 'It's all right,' I told her. 'He's only six, but a sensible lad, he'll find someone and say he's lost and – MIND THAT TRUCK!' When we got there, I sat her down with a large bourbon and went off in search of my son. I asked first at the sweet stall, and they led me straight to him. Finding himself apparently abandoned, he'd gone back to the stall, mentioned he was lost, and they'd called the airport police. The police had taken him down to their office, and by the time I caught up with him he'd learnt the form of arrest, how to use the phone intercom, and how to handcuff the sergeant to the radiator. He was, in short, having a wonderful time, and was very sorry to leave.

Throughout the drama, I was composing in my mind the phone call I'd have to make to you. 'Yes, the show's going splendidly, houses have been wonderful; fine, yes, we're fine, Patrick's fine, Peter Eyre's fine, sends his love, weather's good, hotel's very nice, yes; darling, what I'm really ringing about, you know we used to have *two* sons . . . '

We went to the Capitol, and were allowed to sit in on a Senate session. Somewhat to our disappointment, there were only three people in the chamber. Senator Taft was making a speech about Russian submarine strength; a very old Republican was cleaning out his desk (a rivetting exercise, he kept finding old boiled sweets, broken pencils and bottles of hardened gum, and debating lengthily with himself whether to put them in his attaché case or throw them away), and a very young, very small Senator was acting as Chairman for the day – they do it in rotation – and kept sliding about in his monstrous leather armchair. And that was all.

We had been strictly enjoined not to talk, move, read or cough in the public gallery. But within a few minutes we were joined by several government officials chatting and joking together; parties of schoolchildren came and went, a group of nuns in heavy boots crashed in, got bored and crashed out again; and when we met Taft afterwards I remarked on all this, and he said people never listened to speeches, they just read them afterwards, sometimes, but we had come at a bad time, anyway; things usually got a bit better after lunch.

Visited the Folger Shakespeare Library, which is terrific, and their Elizabethan Theatre, about which I reserve judgment. They were doing *The Tempest*, and although we couldn't stay for a performance, the director proudly ran through the lighting plot for us. It was all surprise pink and peacock blue on a set made of crushed tinfoil. 'I do really think we have the measure of Shakespeare's magic island', he breathed.

The Smithsonian, however, is amazing, and the National Gallery a triumph both of design and content. It's a slightly scary city, though, is Washington, and our respectable WASP area, right by the White House, is apparently the worst for mugging and having your car boarded at traffic lights. There's a kind of surliness, too, a kind of angst, that comes as a shock after California. The stage crew where we are at the National are a kind of parody of militant trade unionism. The floor of our set was badly scratched when it came off the plane – one man with a pot of paint could have put it right in half an hour, but they demanded a full four-hour call with two electricians, two props to move the furniture, a standby carpenter and a painter, and this was just too expensive, so it didn't get done. The O.P. side Props Man only has one job to do the whole evening – pick up my hat and stick from a table, and hand them to me before I go on in Act II. He's never there to do it, because it's boring and unnecessary and he's playing poker. But I'm supposed to wait for him, and, if necessary, call him in time. My suggestion that the hat and stick should be my own responsibility, treated as 'personals', met with an accusation that I was trying to cheat the man out of a job. This sort of nonsense is hard for a good socialist to bear.

Royal York Hotel
Toronto
May 1975

I don't know how our Management have done this, but somehow this hotel not only has no record of our advance booking, but even now after they have found us rooms and we've checked in, they refuse to acknowledge our existence. They can't find our names in the register, won't take messages, and decline to give us our keys. Well, I just keep mine in my pocket permanently, and am pleasantly surprised when I find no-one else installed in my room. Maybe they won't even trace me to give me a bill.

Want to come home now. Been very nice, but enough now. It's terribly cold. And Toronto is full of people in tartan dinner jackets ordering malted milk. Went to Niagara-on-the-Lake yesterday. Weybridge, really. But goodish production of *Pygmalion*, with lovely Beth Shepherd, great to see her again; I have been half in love with easeful Beth. Very good *Two Gents* at Stratford Ontario (Robin Phillips – had lunch with him and we tossed and gored several persons). Went to Montreal, which I loved; after all these weeks of modern streets and concrete office buildings, to see a cobbled square and a genuine 18th-Century portico actually brought tears to my eyes.

The Royal Alexandra is a fine theatre. We are part of a Subscription Season, which means we appear on the list of attractions simply as 'May 5th-24th, GLENDA JACKSON'. No mention of the title, or Ibsen, or the RSC, or Trevor, just Glenda, with keyboard and drums; but we're full, so why worry. There's an interesting Black Theatre company here run by Siobhan Quinlan, who was at Billingham with me. But there's not a lot else. I'm going to New York for a few days when we finish, and home on the 29th.

After Hedda *(we made a film of it, too), I felt a moral obligation to go back to Prospect, who had been asked by Eddie Kulukundis to re-stage the Chichester* Month in the Country *at the Albery. Toby Robertson's production, with Dorothy Tutin and Derek Jacobi, was highly successful, and we tried an experiment in West End Repertoire (always doomed to failure) by running it in tandem with a revival of* A Room with a View, *which I co-directed – if that term has a meaning.*

This, for me, was followed by a rather disappointing year. Derek and I did Staircase, *Charles Dyer's piece about the two gay hairdressers, and it was fun, but nobody was really interested in the play now. I did do* Hard Times *for Granada TV, a wonderful production; and then a rather boring recital tour of Greece, followed by a not very good film in Italy and Germany,* The Devil's Advocate.

Scontrone
L'Aquila
Italy
June 1976

Another gigantic thunderstorm today – the locals are now reluctantly admitting that it does this every June, so massive rescheduling is suddenly called for. To have made the film further south would have meant better weather conditions but also, I'm told, trouble with the Mafia.

I'm writing this sitting in what is supposed to be my church. They're not shooting on me today so I went to look at it before the rain came on, and I'll have to wait for it to stop before I rejoin the Unit at the other end of the village. The priest here could not be more unlike the character I play – he's young, progressive, a closet Communist I think – but at least he can show me how to serve Mass.

There's a bit of a language barrier here, to say the least. Mostly Italian actors, but five British, two German, one French, one Afrikaaner. And Jason Miller, an Irish-American Catholic, is playing the German Jewish Doctor. The one person on the unit who speaks all the necessary languages is reputed to be giving in to a fairly serious nervous breakdown.

My impression, on arriving in Rome, was that the film was being made by a group of middle-aged German ladies in extravagant hats. I was met at the airport by someone called Winny, who said she was deputising for Erika. Erika showed up later, at tea, having had her hair done. Then we were joined by Trudi, who brought my subsistence allowance, and by Kirsten, with a lot of expensive-looking shopping. Nobody spoke about the film, but they all took their shoes off and ordered some champagne, and we had a nice evening.

The next morning, I was driven to the production base at Roccaraso, in the Monti della Meta. Roccaraso is a ski resort, and I expect it really swings during the winter season; in June, however, there is no snow on the mountains and the place is populated by disgruntled hoteliers, unemployed ski instructors and mangy dogs. We're not actually filming in Roccaraso – this village where we're doing so is a little way away, high up, and inaccessible by road when it's wet. Most days we have to climb – the camera car is a donkey, called Iops.

It's all right when you're working, but a dead-and-alive place to be stuck in when you're not. Especially when it's raining. I drive once a week to Rome – 225km – to get decent wine and smokes and books in English for us all, and have to get back the same night even if I'm not supposed to be wanted in the morning, because the schedule's always being altered at the last minute.

We have a few days at Frascati at the end of the month, before going to Munich for the studio stuff. It's not going to be a very good film, but it'll be dead picturesque.

Well, this is a lot better. For us, I mean; the Production Office's failure to check the Italian calendar of religious public holidays – at this time of year there's one for nearly every saint in the canon – has meant we're now probably two weeks behind schedule. The Lutheran fury of our Executive Producer, Dr. Helmut Jedele, is terrible to behold. We could in fact catch up a lot of time by cutting some of the dead wood from the script; John Mills battles manfully with Morris West every night to do this, but doesn't succeed often enough.

This Villa is beautiful. Nearby Frascati is convenient, attractive and full of good restaurants, and Dan Massey and I have decided we have to go for a run every morning to keep in shape. (Don't know how long this will last – it's quite hot, even in the early morning, and anyway we stop and talk.)

I get in to Rome quite a lot, and have seen a number of friends, including Roddy Cavallero of the British Council, who told me he had been in touch with the University after that reading we did at the Goldoni in the spring. Apparently the whole of the English Department were invited, and not one of their 5,000 students turned up. Are they trying to tell us something? This is not the way to cure my paranoia, um, my galloping sensitivity I mean.

I suspect Daniel Massey and I helped to keep each other sane while we were on the film. It's odd how often you're working with someone for the first time in your life, and you find you're with them again on your very next job. Dan and I came home to go straight off to Nottingham to play Othello and Iago for Richard Eyre.

I'm so relieved you think Iago is all right. Some of the press have been enthusiastic, others baffled. Patience Collier liked it, which was cheering, and life is made so awful when she doesn't like something.

It's the only way I can see it. The ability to work on people's feelings is simply a skill – Iago's discovery that he possesses that skill, and can use it with such astounding success, intrigues and captivates him. He exercises it for good (cheering up the company on arrival in Cyprus, comforting Desdemona in Act IV Sc. 2) as well as, upon Othello, for ill; it's the same talent, just used for different purposes. Watching for the effect, predicting the effect, finding his prediction correct, judging how and to what extent to fan the flames further, fascinates him to the exclusion of all else – he is in thrall to his own invention. Morality doesn't come into it, nor does anything else.

So I was depressed the other day when I went to talk to a school group who'd seen it, and they said, 'I thought Iago was supposed to be wicked?' Yes, I said, didn't you think what he did was wicked? Well yes, they said, but you didn't *look* wicked. Oh dear. What do they call Iago, I asked, how do they describe him? Don't know. Honest Iago, I said, they call him *honest* Iago, don't they? Would they do that if he kept twirling his moustaches?

They weren't convinced. And I do have to say that at matinées when Dan is rolling on the ground in his fit, some of the kids do laugh, and that shouldn't happen; something must be wrong. I'm not doing anything – Dan gets furious, what are you doing when I'm having my fit, he asks; come on, show me, I know you're doing something. Honestly Dan, I'm NOT, I tell him; but he doesn't believe me. I gather every Othello and every Iago have this argument. But motiveless evil just is, I think, attractive to the young, and so it's inclined to make them laugh.

Actually I will admit that one night after Othello fatally stabs himself, I did murmur 'Say bye bye Sooty', but ever so quietly.

*When the National Theatre Company moved into its
new home by the Thames, all sorts of companies
moved into the vacated old Vic and did a short stint,
but nothing seemed quite to work.*

*Meanwhile, Prospect was still a homeless peripatetic
company, having to rely on West End managements
whenever they wanted to bring anything into
London; and the Old Vic Theatre seemed by logic
and tradition the appropriate base for their
activities. The Arts Council didn't like the idea, and
it led to serious trouble later; but to me it seemed,
and in retrospect still does seem, the solution both for
theatre and company.*

I was involved in their inaugural 1977 season, in
Hamlet *(Derek Jacobi, Barbara Jefford), Christopher
Logue's* War Music *and* Antony and Cleopatra *(Alec
McCowen and Dorothy Tutin). After the Vic, we
toured the UK, Germany and the Middle East.*

Being charged with getting these three productions into the different venues means I'm confronted each day by a new and totally unexpected set of problems. When we did *Hamlet* at Rumelar Hissar Castle in Istanbul, a curiously un-Danish note was struck by the Muezzins. The courtyard of the Doge's Palace at Dubrovnik seemed ideal for a performance, until about ten thousand sleeping starlings saw the stage lights come on, thought it was dawn and sang lustily for the next three hours, during which time nobody heard a word. Industrial action at Lubljana Airport meant that the skips containing the wigs, swords and armour failed to arrive, so characters had to go to war unwigged and unarmed.

Here at Split, we have a new difficulty. We're playing on the steps of the fine Palace of Diocletian, and it looks wonderful. The only thing is, that if you make an exit on one side of the stage and have to re-enter from the other, you have to go down some steps to a courtyard, along a narrow public alleyway into a side street, and back into the palace by a side entrance. This you have to do with some speed. Last night, Andrew Sear, in a bulky robe, got as far as the alleyway, and to his horror saw a very fat Yugoslavian coming in the other direction. 'Back up, back up!' he yelled, but the man pressed on, impassably, muttering his rights. Andrew did what any resourceful actor would in the circumstances: he drew his sword, and the man turned and ran, screaming.

When you join us in Jordan, where we're playing at the Palace of Culture in Amman (actually a 6,000 seat basketball stadium) there will be new worries.

But don't get the idea that there haven't been tremendous compensations dramatically. In Istanbul at the beginning of *War Music* I had the whole cast coming up from the shore and over the hill, in single file, carrying flaming torches which Stephen had somehow borrowed from the Turkish National Theatre, and it looked extraordinary in the moonlight. In Hamlet at Lovrejenac Castle, we couldn't think where to put John Turner for his first Ghost appearance, and he gamely offered to go right up to the very top of the keep, and stand on the wall seventy feet above our heads. We were able to isolate him with light, as if he were standing in the sky.

Hamlet is very well known here, it is performed in Dubrovnik every year by a young actor who has become friends with Derek, and our own production has gone down well. *Antony* they're not so sure about. *War Music* they treat as a romp. I love Yugoslavia, and we have made a lot of friends, both Serb and Croat. I have also fallen passionately for the double bass player in the Women's Quintette at the Cafe Brsalje in Dubrovnik, but alas I'm told she is spoken for by the violist. I daresay I shall get over it in time.

Another rather dispiriting year. A film, Agatha, *which didn't quite work. A play at the Royal Court,* Laughter *by Peter Barnes, which came off a week early by popular request. A revival of* The Homecoming *at the Garrick, the respectful reviews for which nevertheless failed to promote much activity at the box office. As Arthur Askey used to say, 'The notices are fine, it's the word of mouth that's killing us.' Anyway, two days before we closed, the 'House Full' board was brought out, covered in cobwebs, from the cellar where it had lain since we opened, and very ostentatiously scrubbed down in order to be of service for the next show,* Deathtrap.

Next for me, Cardinal Wolsey in the BBC TV Shakespeare Henry VIII. *One of the best productions in the whole series, but of course it's the play nobody wants to know about. And so to a recital tour (again Prospect, by now calling itself the Old Vic Company) to Hong Kong and all over Australia: the actors were Isla Blair, Derek Jacobi, Julian Glover and me, there were three musicians, and Michael Redington came with us as Manager.*

In the air, near Jakarta
February 1979

It's 1 a.m. on the Cathay Pacific Flight from Hong Kong to Perth. The cabin staff are officially on strike, but the plane couldn't legally fly without them, even though they're not actually working, and they wanted to go to Perth anyway. All except one, who only wanted to go as far as Jakarta, but that would have meant his mates getting stranded there too, so a certain amount of pressure was brought to bear on the poor man, and we flew on.

So we're on the last leg of the journey – we've moved ourselves up into the First Class section, and the catering and bar services have been franchised out to the Old Vic Company. I'm attempting to warm up the Foo Yong while Michael Redington demonstrates the safety equipment and Julian runs the bar. On the flight deck the crew seem to be up to strength, I'm happy to say. I made a sandwich for the captain and took it in to him, and had a nice chat. His co-pilot used to be Third Horn for the National Youth Orchestra. Ellie, our Stage Manager. has made some salad, and is now asking the non-operative stewards (who are still travelling Tourist I'm afraid) how to make the coffee. They won't actually tell her, but have agreed to nod or shake their heads in answer to specific questions.

Well, Hong Kong. It grows on one, but then it has to, because on arrival the jet-lag, humidity and fog combine to hit you with a feeling of sloth and depression that lasts fully five days. The squeezed, vertical nature of the island doesn't help, nor does the consciousness that pretty well everything you see, eat, walk into or sleep on belongs either to Swires or Jardine Matheson.

But good things too. The harbour, the ferries, the trams, the outlying islands, the country up towards the Chinese border. We've done a bit of sailing, and I've bought you quite a lot of silk, and eaten some delicious Cantonese food, and been to a monastery, and seen some disgusting poverty, which is joyously displayed as a tourist attraction. We've had lunch with the Governor and his wife, and been very hospitably looked after by the Jockey Club, and by a group of influential Cantonese ladies.

One night of Suzie-Wongery in Kowloon, with topless waitresses dropping cigarette ash on their nipples, convinced me they do this sort of thing better in Stockport.

Park Towers Hotel
Perth, W. A.,
1979

It's not like the Hong Kong Hilton, but it's matey, and Western Australia is warm, welcoming and attractive. Very good Festival, run by Sheffield-born ex-General Manager of the Bournemouth Symphony Orchestra, David Blenkinsop. Not more than 1.2 million souls in the whole vast area of Western Australia, and internal air fares are so high that it's as cheap to fly from Sydney to Athens as it is from Sydney to Perth, so it's amazing that a Festival as large as this can survive at all. Everybody goes to everything, and gives parties afterwards. Tom Stoppard is here as official guest-of-honour, which was a very nice surprise. They did a late-night production of *After Magritte* for his benefit and I went with him to hold his hand.

The city is just about 150 years old (Colonel Light, 1836) and very spacious. Like Adelaide, the suburbs of one-storey houses and little gardens stretch for miles and miles without adding much to the population figures. The River Swan, broad and always full of yachts, flows through the city and out into the sea at Fremantle. The Regal Cinema, where we're playing, is not among the beauties of Perth. Paddy, the manager, until recently used to go round the countryside with a motor-bike and side-car, doing fit-up film shows in halls, sports centres, and I'm afraid mostly bars. The films were short and in black and white, and were called things like *Hetty's Little Ways*, *Girls at the Gynaecologists* and *A Surprise for Alison*.

There's a large soundproof room at the back of the auditorium, labelled CRYING ROOM. Mothers attending the Saturday morning Film Show leave their babies in there with an attendant while they watch the picture. Each baby is given a number, and when it cries the relevant number is conveyed to Paddy in the projection box, and he flashes it on the screen so that the mother can go and attend to her child. Brilliant idea. I suggested it could be adapted for our own use, and that Ellie, perhaps in a sequinned costume and pink tights, could come on to the stage holding aloft an illuminated numeral as necessary, but in fact in the evenings the mothers tend to bring their offspring in with them, and feed them during the performance.

Derek and I went off to Cottesloe Beach to swim yesterday, but when we got there it was surprisingly cold, so we went for a walk along the sands instead, and looked for some unusual shells for Derek to take back to Brenda Bruce, who has a collection.

We must have walked quite a long way, because without realising it we had strayed on to the next beach north, which is reserved for nude bathing, customarily male. Suddenly, my downward gaze met a large pair of bronzed feet, followed, as I looked up, by the unencumbered appurtenances of their owner. 'Can I help you gentlemen?' he demanded rather than enquired.

Derek's face turned beetroot. 'No, thankyou,' he stammered, 'We were just looking for sea-shells for a friend.'

It was perhaps not the most fortunate of utterances, and our naked companion considered it for some while before making a reply. 'All right,' he said at last. 'But keep moving.' And he rejoined his friends. I turned to go back the way we came, but Derek grabbed me by the arm. 'No, no!' he hissed. 'If we go back, they'll think we only came to spy on them. We've got to keep walking!'

'But, Derek,' I reasoned, 'if we go on walking north, we've got to walk right round Australia, and we've got a matinée at four.'

'We'll find some way of getting back,' he said urgently. 'Now come on.'

So we went on, with carefully downcast eyes, picking up a few shells, until we were out of the Realm of Adonis, and then doubled back through the undergrowth, dodging the snakes and funnel-web spiders and blue-ringed octopuses and other hazards with which the robust Australians decorate their beaches, until we finally got back to the car.

Made A$360 on a treble on the 'trots' today at Ascot (Perth), by a total fluke; I had no views at all about any horse in the place. They didn't have enough in the Tote to pay me, and had to take me down to an underground vault for it, with armed guards. I felt terribly important.

Don Dunstan has just resigned as Premier of South Australia. He was in such a state of grief after his young wife's death that he said he was just not capable of carrying on. I'm going to see him next week. I don't know much about Mr. Constable, his successor, but Don will be a hard act to follow. The superiority of the educational system in this State, the social services, Aboriginal development, and cultural provision, are all pretty well due to him. The actors, dancers and musicians here, particularly, are inconsolable.

The news we get of Britain suggests you're all on the point of moral, physical and economic collapse. Though the suggestion is put with considerable local glee, so it may well be exaggerated. Teachers on strike, eh. Tom McDonnell, out here with S. A. Opera, says his children at Highgate haven't been to school for a month, and won't go now till Easter. Don't tell Joe, he'll want us to move to Highgate.

The audiences here are pleased to see us, but it's the old situation of coming abroad with what, however you dress them up, is essentially a series of readings/recitals/ 'entertainments', and everyone saying, 'very nice, yes, but why didn't you bring a play?' Particularly so in this very fine but not very intimate Festival Theatre. We feel we're cheating them a bit. The Byron really does get them though, and Derek has them all awash by the end, even the hardened old pro's who are playing elsewhere in the Festival.

I suppose in 1979 British television drama was about as good as it has ever been. Crime and Punishment *and* Churchill and the Generals, *in both of which I took part that year, were superbly made – and expensive – productions for a BBC at the top of its creative bent.*

Then I did a not-so-wonderful film with Burt Reynolds, whom I liked, entitled Rough Cut, *and went to California to play the Roman Emperor Vespasian in* Masada *– one of those pictures where all the good guys (in this case the Jews) are played by Americans, and the bad guys (the Romans) by the Brits, because we're good at dialogue, and the Romans had more to say.*

Beecham *– an entertainment about the renowned conductor and wit – at the Apollo Theatre was fun, not least because of the number of musicians who had played under him that came round every night after the show – we'd open a bottle of Scotch and they'd tell me more and more stories about the old boy, many of which went into the script.*

The show was a short but peaceful voyage in untroubled waters, prior to my being hit by the storms which I could see developing as soon as I was asked by the Old Vic Board to take over as Artistic Director. The next eighteen months were a struggle, financial and otherwise.

We 'bought in' productions for an initial period, played two seasons of our own repertoire at the Vic and around the UK, and then took our Merchant of Venice *on an extensive tour of Europe.*

82

Teatro del'Arte
Milan
May 1981

I was at a dress rehearsal of *Figaro* at la Scala, to which the Company had been invited, when someone brought me a telegram. I opened it and read the words: OLD VIC COMPANY BANKRUPT AS FROM TODAY PLEASE RING REGARDS – ANDREW

Well, we knew it was on the cards. Ever since the Arts Council peremptorily withdrew our whole grant rather late in the day, the battle to continue has been a losing one. Our hope was that our creditors would agree to what is called a 'composition' – that is, they would allow us to continue trading so as to earn income to pay them off at a reasonable rate in the pound. But they didn't so agree, and so that's it. Of course we are permitted to continue with our present tour, which is booked out in Brussels, Eindhoven, Ludwighsaven, The Hague, Rotterdam, Arnhem, Wiesbaden, Zurich, Luxembourg and Copenhagen already. It's ironic that the Company's swansong, a production that was substituted at the last minute for *Macbeth*, should have been so eagerly welcomed by eight European countries, while at home they're busy chopping us up for firewood.

Starting off the tour in Italy has meant a bit of a baptism of fire for our staff. The Teatro del'Arte is one of a group owned by the Piccolo Milano, very antiquated with no proper fly-lines, just a series of ropes and pulleys tied off on the gantry handrail. Very little FOH lighting. Nobody speaks English, and they don't like cue-lights. Consequently our Stage Management have all had to learn Italian, of a sort. For Teresa, on the book, having to give all the cues to the resident crew, this is particularly vital. The show relay mike is on her prompt desk, so in the dressing room you don't hear much of the show; what you hear is Teresa:

'Attenzione Mario, Vittorio and Enrico. Flies cue un-dice, electrice cue dodice, VIA. Oh fuck. Vittorio, wrong direzzione. ARRETE! Up again. Oh well. Hey, Trev, how are we going to get the table off? He's left it outside the house. Tell David to take it off with him when he goes. Bloody hell. OW! Mario, stop that, leave me alone. I *mean* it. All right, will you stop if I lend you my hat? Yeh, you look lovely. Molto bello. What? Oh yes ATTEN-ZIONE Giuseppe movare il truck della casa di Shylock NOT YET oh Jesus wait till I say *via* . . .' and so on. Nevertheless the Milanese audiences lap it up, and the language bar-rier stimulates a directness and clarity in some of the per-formances which have become a little decorative of late.

I haven't yet told the Company the bad news, but I'll have to make an announcement in a day or two, before they hear it through the bush telegraph. The people I'm most upset about are the wonderful office and produc-tion staff back at the Vic, who, having cleared the colos-sal inherited deficit are now hard at work planning our next season – now to no purpose.

On Wednesday we took the train to Como, and the Lake steamer up to Bellagio; the weather balmy, the gardens of the Villa Melzi top-heavy with azaleas and rhododendrons. No sound but the bees. So much beauty all around. Can we really be only 800 miles from the Waterloo Road?

Tivoli Concert Hall
Copenhagen
June 1981

Fourteen hour train-and-boat journey from Strasbourg, but more pleasurable I think than the flight. Breakfast at the Mission Hotel, where we're staying, is surprising; a young very fat man with long greasy hair and pebble glasses and an oatmeal coloured terylene suit plays the ORGAN. A selection from *Oklahoma* as you munch your muesli.

Very nice Publicity Manager at the Tivoli got David and me tickets for *Tosca* at the Theatre Royal. Danish Opera Company. The tenor sang in Italian, everybody else in Danish, which produced a curious effect in the Third Act duets with Tosca, singing the same words together in two different languages. I learned that if you're Danish, then you have to sing in Danish, but visiting artists have the freedom not to. So I assumed the tenor was Italian, till I looked at the programme and found out he was actually Swedish. Scandinavian one-upmanship. The production had that unmistakable air of having been in the repertoire for some time. The Scarpia was, I think, drunk, and didn't stay for the curtain call. Spoletta made it quite clear that he was used to singing much larger parts, and knocked over quite a lot of monks and blind people in the first act to show Power. The relationship between the Sacristan and the choirboys was one that seemed liable to develop fruitfully in the dressing room. Orchestra very good, they play in shirt-sleeves, indeed nobody dresses up much, and the seats are terribly cheap.

High taxes on personal property here go to social services, health, transport, sport, education, culture (the subsidy to box office ratio at the Theatre Royal is 9:1) and unemployment benefit. This last is payable at 90 per cent of your last salary, and critics of the economy argue reasonably that when you add what you save on fares and meals, you're better off not working. A lot of the kids don't work, they wander around Copenhagen carrying bottles of beer and getting very belligerent in the evenings. At a very good party given by our lady Ambassador, we met the Arts Minister, also responsible for Sport, extremely bright; 'We have a big leisure problem,' she said, 'and we must make sure there are interesting things for them to do that don't cost them very much.' It sounds so simple put like that.

Teatro Valli
Rome
June 1981

The curtain has just fallen on the last performance by the Old Vic Company. This is not the unique event that it sounds; of course there have been other last performances by other Old Vic Companies, more distinguished ones; we're just the company that was running the Old Vic at the time, and doing the overseas classical touring with which that name has traditionally been associated.

After every performance we've given on this tour, when I've made a speech about the closure of the company, what I'm met with is blank incredulity. When I tell them about the Arts Council cutting 41 organisations this year for a total saving of 1.4 million pounds, they think I've got it wrong, that I must have moved the decimal point. Dr. Doll, the intendant of the Wurtembergisches Staatstheater, was baffled. 'But that's what I get in one year for my theatre and opera house here in Stuttgart', he told me. Thousands of people have signed a petition to be presented to our Arts Minister, not that it will do any good.

And who knows what will happen to the poor old theatre itself? It so badly needs the attention that only love and a great deal of money can provide.

Well, I mustn't sit here in the dressing room getting maudlin. I'm only writing this because, having packed my make-up, there's nothing else to do. No one's come round, we went out not with a bang but a whimper. This was the least successful date on the tour; Rome is a funny place, nobody knows what's on. Some of the cast are going out on the Town on their last night – I don't feel like it. I gave lunch at Passetto to Neil and Ros and Richard and David and Lynne and some of the others who have been with us since the start, to say thank you for the work and the loyalty and the friendship. Tomorrow we'll all get on the plane, and at Heathrow we'll say goodbye and go our several ways. I can't even go in and clear out my office – the Liquidator's already done that.

*If at first you don't succeed, try something totally
different. A good maxim, I think; and when, after
the traumas of the Old Vic, I received an invitation
to come and work as Director-in-Residence for a
term at the beautiful University of Western Australia,
I accepted with alacrity and relief. The major play I
decided to work on with the students was
Middleton's* Women Beware Women.

*While I was there, it was agreed that Pru should join
me and when term was over that she should direct
me in* Uncle Vanya *for the W. A. National Theatre
Company in Perth.*

The University is a pleasure to work in. I have a good-sized study with a beautiful view; it's cool and shady and the bookshelves have been stocked with love and discrimination, and a peacock comes and sits on my window-sill. The Faculty are extremely friendly, and my cleaning lady calls me 'Professor'.

I've been given a perfectly OK apartment temporarily but it's nothing to the lovely house they're arranging for when you all come out. Tell the boys there are invitations stacked up for swimming, tennis, riding, table tennis, sailing and cricket. I think they'll manage.

I go on being fascinated by the modernity of *Women Beware Women*, and particularly by the characters of the four women themselves. It fits so easily into a present-day setting that I'm sure I must be doing something terribly wrong. The cast are receptive and very intelligent but, at present, wanting something of a spark. I just hope it doesn't turn out like so many of my productions: super-detailed, severely truthful and dull as a dead bee.

In my spare moments I'm casting *Vanya* for you. Edgar Metcalfe will play Astrov as agreed, Nita Pannell Marina. There's a problem about Yelyena. They absolutely have no money to bring an actress over from Sydney or Melbourne, and I really have found nobody here as yet who's remotely right. I've made them understand your stipulation about Sonia that she shouldn't be the prettiest actress in the company with her hair scraped back and no eye make-up, and I'm seeing a couple of promising girls tomorrow.

The very nice people at the Tourist Office have rather taken me under their wing, and have arranged for me to go with the boys down a working gold mine in Kalgoorlie. But not you, I'm afraid, women positively not allowed. Maybe it's the miners' language, or maybe they tried it once and the aphrodisiac properties of the gold stimulated some untoward behaviour, I just don't know.

A script has arrived from Granada for a series called *Brass*. It's a send up of every North-of-England image that's ever been evoked by pen, brush or camera, and it made me laugh so much I fell out of bed. The producer and director are fighting hard not to have to do it in front of a studio audience, which would indeed be fatal. It has to look very real, and go very fast. I know you go along fairly happily with the studio sit-com tradition, but I really hate it. The basis of television is that it is watched by three or four people at a time, and however much they laugh at a joke, you should be able to push on with the action without fear of their losing the next line. But to have to hang around while two hundred and fifty people in the studio laugh – what does the poor vision mixer do? Stay on the person who's made the joke, while he or she makes an extra face to fill in time? Or cut early to someone else, who then has to keep a heavy reaction going until the laughter dies?

And anyway, isn't comedy funnier if you believe it? How can you explain the presence of those 250 unseen laughers? Where are they, behind the sofa? Under the drinks table? Outside those French windows, that always have net curtains to save the trouble of painting a backing?

Is it to show people it's meant to be funny? Can't they tell? After all, in Drama you don't have to hear 250 people crying, to tell you when it's sad. Dear oh dear.

I'm sorry to hear about the continuing disaster of the car. I wrote a full and quite polite letter to Renault's, but have not had a reply. Nobody here to whom I mention it is at all surprised, but then they all buy Holdens. A Holden will stay together for three years, and if it goes wrong, you punch the man on the nose who sold it to you. They do these things properly out here.

In 1982 I played Mr. Bumble in a new film version of Oliver Twist, *starring George C. Scott as a rather gentlemanly Fagin, and made, as I remember it, in a damp shed in Luton. Well, my bits, anyway.*

Then it was Brass *for Granada, a wonderful teamwork effort by every single person involved, and possibly the happiest job of my life. We recorded the shows in Manchester. but rehearsed in London, at the Oval. Of course, now that I was working, for a change, a couple of miles from home, Pru immediately got a job in Australia.*

Midland Hotel
Manchester
November 1982

Coming up yesterday, a businessman and, I think, his
P.A. – who may also have been his wife – joined the
train at Watford Junction. The conversation went like
this:

SHE: So why won't you consider Stuart?
HE: Well, he didn't present well at interview, did he?
   In the first place, he was half an hour late.
SHE: He lost his way. He explained that.
HE: He's not computer-literate. His arithmetic is terrible.
   He can't spell. There's nothing in his background to
   suggest he'd be at all suitable for either job.
SHE (*sulky*): You just don't like him.
HE: I don't *dis*like him. I just don't want him in my office.
SHE: He very kindly drove us to the station!
HE: And went the wrong way down a one-way street.
SHE (*after a pause*): That's because you made him
   nervous.
   (*Silence, until Stoke-on-Trent.*)

The Publicity people arranged for me to have lunch with
Joe Gormley and his wife. I've admired him for so long,
and it was such a pleasure to meet them both. He told
me how he became politically involved with the miners'

cause in the thirties: very reluctantly, it was. The agitators left him cold, his only concern was that the men should see more of their wives and children. His wife was a member of the Socialist Women's Group in 1932, and I asked him how they met. He said he fell in love with her when he heard her sing solos in Chapel. I asked, had she a wonderful voice? 'That woman,' said Joe, his eyes shining, 'had the musical aptitude of a ball of wool. I felt so sorry for her, I thought I'd better marry her.'

Love to all in Melbourne. If you have problems finding somewhere to eat after the show, remember the Waiters' Club, round the corner from the Princess. It's down an alley, up a dark stairway, incredibly tatty and probably the centre for all kinds of organised crime, but the food is OK and they're open all night. It's popular with the opera people, who call it Sparafucile's.

At the end of the first series of Brass, *I was sent a
play by Justin Greene, at the Leicester Haymarket,*
Master Class, *by David Pownall, A brilliant play,
about an imaginary meeting between Stalin,
Prokofiev and Shostakovitch during the infamous
Russian Musicians' Conference of 1947. A grand
piano, which I subsequently bought from the
management, stood at the centre of the stage, and
we had a musically talented cast: Peter Kelly as
Prokofiev, David Bamber as Shostakovitch, and
Jonathan Adams as Zhdanov, the Cultural Minister.*

The Cottage at Uppingham
February 1983

Leicestershire is thick with snow. Looks absolutely beautiful, BUT going home last Thursday night, left the theatre
11.00, quite a lot of snow falling; when we reached the
high ground it was blowing across the road quite hard
and banking up against the hedgerows. About three
miles from the Uppingham turn, the traffic in front came
to a dead stop, for no visible reason. Nothing coming the
other way either. I could see the lights of cars through
the snow and beyond the trees, stretching up the hill
and over to the south for more than a mile. Time passed.
Drivers switched off their engines, then their lights. It
was silent and dark, and began to get very cold indeed.
Radio 2 told us, repeatedly, on no account to go out in
our cars, particularly in Leicestershire.

Snow began to build up rapidly round each vehicle. It
was already too late to get out and walk, the drifts were
too deep, there was no moon, and it was that stretch of
the road furthest from any human habitation. I ran the
engine to get the benefit of the heater, but I wasn't sure
I had enough petrol to keep it running all night.

At 5.30 a.m. two arctic policemen in snow-shoes appeared out of the darkness, prised us out of our cars, and
took us down a path they'd dug, to where they had
some Land Rovers with chained wheels, and drove us into
Uppingham. Non-residents were put up at the Falcon

and told they'd be taken back to their vehicles as soon as the snow-plough arrived. I left my number with the sergeant, who promised to phone me, and clambered away to the cottage.

Well, he didn't, and when I woke at nine after two hours' sleep and rang the station, they said the plough had been and gone, and people had driven away. So I walked four miles back to the mountain of snow inside which I hoped I'd find my car – of course, as it passed by, the snow-plough had hurled a great deal of snow underneath the chassis, so that it was resting on a solid block of packed ice. I trudged a mile back to the nearest house to try and borrow a spade, but the most they had was a small coal-shovel. However, I worked with this for three hours, and finally freed the car and unfroze the door. A police car came by while I was digging, and they promised to notify the theatre in case I couldn't get the car started; but eventually I did, and drove very slowly towards Leicester.

That ought to have been the end of the story, but it wasn't. On the road I was overtaken by an old orange Hillman, and a man got out and said he was Andy Gordon from the Haymarket Publicity office, and that he had arranged for an RAF Rescue helicopter to bring me in from Uppingham. I said thanks very much, most flat- tered, but I've had very little sleep and a hard morning and now I'm already half way to Leicester all I want to do is carry on and get to the dressing room for a kip before the show. No, no, he said, you don't understand, this is essential, there are two TV crews waiting at Leicester Racecourse to see you arrive, you've got to come back to Uppingham.

We found a phone box and rang the theatre and I said it just wasn't on, and they were terribly unhappy about it. And then we found that Andy's car wouldn't start, and he said what am I going to do, *I've* got to get back to Uppingham anyway, to apologise to the pilot. There was absolutely no traffic on the road from which he could beg a lift, so, furious, I rang the theatre back and told them I'd do it after all, and drove him back to Uppingham. On the way I said, you do know where we're going, don't you? I could immediately tell that he didn't, but he answered, 'I think it'll be Uppingham School.'

The School Sergeant made it clear to us that he knew nothing about a helicopter, and that if such a phenomenon were to materialise within the precincts, he would be the very first to be informed. I asked him where were the school playing fields. There were some in one place, some in another. We drove to the first, found nothing, and were on our way to the second when Andy remarked that it was now twenty minutes past pick-up time, so the helicopter would have gone now and we might as well get back to Leicester.

I wondered whether to hit him now, or wait till I'd had some sleep and then hit him harder. I decided on the latter course. On our way back we stopped at his car, which started immediately. When I got to the theatre, the rest of the publicity staff were waiting, reproachfully, in the foyer. There had been a helicopter, somewhere, and it had flown back to Leicester empty, and the RAF were very angry at having their time wasted. I was a spoilsport. I got through the evening show by pretending Shostakovitch was Andy Gordon. David was terribly frightened, and played lots of wrong notes.

Haymarket
Leicester
February 1983

I think the show is in good shape, and there is talk of a transfer. I can't do it until next year, of course, because of more *Brass* – don't know if it'll keep that long.

Had a splendid interview on Friday with local Radio, in the dressing room. Went like this:

INTERVIEWER: Look, before we start I've got to confess, I'm supposed to have *seen* the play. I was meant to come on Tuesday, but you know how it is Timothy, one of the lads had a birthday, and there we were in the pub, and I looked at my watch and I said, Christ, I'm supposed to be at the Leicester Haymarket! So I'm going to talk to you as if I'd seen the play, all right? Testing testing Mary had a little lamb one two three four five. Good evening Timothy West, and what brings you to Leicester in this powerful Socialist Political Drama, *Master Class*?

ME: It's not a Socialist Political Drama.

INTERVIEWER: What?

ME: It's not a political drama at all. It's a very funny play about music.

INTERVIEWER: Well, yes, Yes! Yes, it is, a *very* funny play. In parts.

ME: At least, *I* think so.

INTERVIEWER: Yes, you're right, it is. I mean, it *is* a political drama; but there are, also, some funny – *bits* – in it. Right?

ME: Right.

INTERVIEWER: For instance.

ME: What?

INTERVIEWER: For instance?

ME: Mm? Oh! Yes, well, I think the Composition scene in Act II is a brilliant piece of comic writing.

INTERVIEWER: Yes! The Composition scene! That really had me rolling in the aisles!

ME: And people seem to enjoy –

INTERVIEWER: The Composition scene is hilarious!

ME: Yes? Good. What I was going to say –

INTERVIEWER: That Composition scene is a hoot.

ME: Just because Stalin appears in the play, it doesn't mean –

INTERVIEWER: And?

ME: – that the play is necessarily to do with – what did you say?

INTERVIEWER: *And?*

ME: And what?

INTERVIEWER: And you ALL PLAY THE PIANO! (*Terrible doubt.*) Don't you?

ME: Well, yes, we do. I mean the other three play properly; I play like I think Stalin might have played.

INTERVIEWER: Ha ha! REALLY BADLY!

ME (*nettled*): Well, the point is, he only had the use of one hand –

INTERVIEWER: Timothy, you're a member of the Royal Shakespeare Company –

ME: No, I'm not.

INTERVIEWER: Aren't you? Well, you've done a lot of Shakespeare, anyway, haven't you, and heavy stuff generally, and we all remember you as Henry . . .

ME: Henry who?

INTERVIEWER: King Henry.

ME: King Edward.
INTERVIEWER: I meant Edward. Edward the Eighth.
ME: No, I'm sorry, the Seventh.
INTERVIEWER (*now tired and very bored*): Timothy West,
thank you very much.

No, I know I shouldn't have given him a bad time, but
really . . . Why does the Henry/Edward thing annoy me
so much? It happens all the time. Last week it cropped
up again, and I endeavoured to correct the man, but he
corrected me. 'No, Henry the Eighth it was,' he said
firmly. 'Have it your own way,' I told him. It's disappointing, not only that in thirteen episodes I failed to
convey to viewers even the name of my character, but,
more importantly, disappointing in what it indicates
about popular apprehension of history. Anything that
isn't current is Yesterday; and as, therefore, the Battle of
the Somme might well have been fought with bows and
arrows, and King Alfred's cakes burnt in the preparations
for the Boston Tea Party, it wouldn't be surprising to find
Bluff King Hal driving to Epsom in a de Dion Bouton, or
Bertie in doublet-and-hose attending executions on
Tower Green.

For some years, I'd been a rather inactive member of ACTER, an organisation of British performers (mostly ex-RSC) who tour round American universities, doing plays, teaching, giving workshops on English (mainly classical) drama. They called on me now for a quick visit to California.

Santa Barbara, Ca.
March 1983

I'm in a beautiful house in the hills above Santa Barbara, belonging to Margaret Mallory. Some splendid pictures, and a rather self-opinionated black cat called Pola Negri who, when she desires to enter a room, lifts a front paw and bangs on the door like a postman. She's quite fat, and eats everything, except mice.

I'm here with Tony Church and a six-month-pregnant Lisa Harrow to do a programme (with Martin Best and Ann Firbank who drove up from L.A.) to raise grants for Californian students to attend British Drama Schools.

Very exciting weather – California's worst in living memory – there was a tornado in Los Angeles, and torrential rain and twenty-foot waves in the harbour here, destroying piers and wharves and washing expensive houses into the sea. The hillsides are pouring liquid mud.

Everyone in the district who has a large house that hadn't yet disappeared down the hill, arranged a brunch party for yesterday morning, with telescopes provided, trained out to sea. The occasion was the arrival of the Royal Yacht, and the bringing ashore of the Queen and her party for lunch at the Reagans' ranch. Each hostess, as the weather worsened, was rung up by the White House to say would they please cancel their parties and stand ready to give the Queen lunch if she couldn't get up the hill to the Reagans. Bollocks, they said. In the end, the yacht couldn't put to sea at all, and Reagan flew them up in his private plane. They had a country Mexican lunch of red beans and enchilladas in his ranch house, and Her Majesty suddenly found it necessary to return to Long Beach before dinner, in case she got the same thing again, micro-waved. Or so it was reported to me by a distinguished local Democrat, hugging herself with glee.

While all this was going on, we were erecting our own rostra, rigging our own lighting and rehearsing our show, in the capacious country residence of an oil magnate who provides jars of jelly beans in every room in case the President should drop by. Two hundred and fifty stolid millionaires came to the performance, were fed Californian champagne and nine different sorts of cake, and talked through most of the first half; but they were silent later, and declared it the most wonderful thing they had ever heard, which I suppose it may have been.

Dame Judith Anderson aged 84 was there, being a local resident, and amid general consternation announced that she was going to perform the letter scene from *Macbeth*. And she did, all the parts, Macbeth, servant and all; and it was highly intelligent, most exciting, ringingly clear and splendidly fast. She got a huge ovation, and then Annie Firbank gave her two enormous vodkas, one in each hand, and she drank them and went to sleep.

I'm going back to L.A. tomorrow, though it's lovely here or would be but for the rain. I want to find myself a new American agent; my present one just tells you how terrible everything is and then falls off his bar-stool.

For a long time I'd been trying to take Beecham *to Australia, but failed because an actor over there had been performing an earlier version of the script, and doing it very successfully. But we did get an offer to take it to New Zealand, and with my co-performer Terry Wale, I flew off to Auckland in November.*

Chateau Regency
Christchurch
November 1983

It's a long flight. Arrived in Auckland at 11 a.m. on Saturday. As we drove from the airport Terry was rather
silent, and then said: 'What I can't understand is how
we've flown thirteen thousand miles, and we're still in
Thames Ditton.'

Did a Press Conference, then an Official lunch, then
back to the airport to fly to Wellington; press interview,
radio chat show, dinner with the management, then to
TV studios to make a commercial for the tour. The only
time I've ever gone to sleep making-up.

Wellington is an attractive city, wooden houses – some
of them huge – painted in pastel colours, and a hilly
residential area with a fine view along the coast. Two
aerosol graffiti opposite the hotel proclaimed DESTRUCTIVE
ADOLECENTS (sic) and CRUTCHLESS KNICKERS!!! (their exclam-
ation marks). Sunday was devoted to more interviews
(advance booking apparently very poor), and rehearsals
for the televised N.Z. Music Awards, at which I was to
present the Classical Music Award and also do a bit of
Beecham.

The newly constructed Michael Fowler Hall was festooned in Miralex, and musicians were everywhere.
Apart from three categories, the fare to be adjudicated
was a simple mixture of hard rock and mid-70s video

pop. The exceptions were a jazz award, the Maori award, and the classical one. There were four nominations in this final category: Kiri te Kanawa, for practically anything you care to name, the NZ Youth Choir for a single entitled 'Royal Occasion', an Auckland vocal group doing a Swingles act, and a lady called Louise who sings a number called 'Louise' and it counts as Classical because she's backed by a section of the New Zealand Symphony Orchestra. (They, by the way, are lovely people, and they're sponsoring our tour, poor benighted fools.) Kiri te Kanawa won, natch. The presentation was lit generously in pink and purple, and I shared a dressing room with someone called Hogsnort Rupert.

Yesterday's headline in 'The Dominion': 'Lange (Labour Party leader) Says Muldoon Tells Lies'. Today's headline: 'Muldoon Says Lange Tells Lies'. The sophisticated cut-and-thrust of New Zealand politics is a little dazzling till you get used to it.

This morning we flew down to Christchurch, where we open on Thursday. We are going tonight to the Court Theatre to see *London Assurance*, directed by Elric Hooper; and were intrigued to see advertised at the Court's Studio a play by Harold Pinter quite unknown to either of us. Further research revealed that the play is in fact the work of a local critic called Harold POINTER. Leaving out the 'o' accidentally on purpose must give a useful boost to the box office, as well as encouragement to those unrecognised dramatists John Oosborne, Simon Goray and Michael O'Frayn.

Hope the Tricycle play is going well, and give my love to Oolwen Woymark.

There are aspects of theatrical practice here which strike Terry and me as a little unorthodox. We were only doing four performances in Christchurch, opening on Thursday to a small but very appreciative house, and on Friday morning there was a splendid local review. However Friday was a regional holiday, so the box office, which is in the Town Hall and not the theatre, was closed. It was closed on Saturday as well (like everything else in Christchurch: the only way you can tell the difference between Saturday and Sunday is that on Sunday the churches are open), and on Monday we were gone.

We hired a car, and drove up to Picton on the tip of the South Island – a beautiful day, breathtaking scenery, gorgeous wild flowers. Left the car, and got on the boat for Wellington – a three-and-a-half-hour sail. We were adopted at once by the very nice Liverpudlian purser, who took us up to the wardroom for quite a lot of whisky. First Officer also a Cheshire man and very charming – Second Officer Welsh and sang under Beecham at Llandaff. The Captain and Chief Engineer about the only Kiwis on the ship. The Captain was amazing: lots of curly hair, no front teeth, extremely camp, falling about with high-pitched laughter. He took us up to the bridge to watch him perform what I'd just read was the most difficult piece of navigation in New Zealand: getting through the rocky entrance of the Cook Sound into the open sea against a six-knot current, keeping to an extremely narrow channel festooned with crayfishing buoys. This he discharged in fits of giggles, waving his arms like a windmill.

'Starboard fifteen,' he sang out. 'I hope. What do I usually do here, John? Oh, I don't know. Well, here goes. It might be all right. Midships. That always sounds good, doesn't it?' Did it beautifully, of course. Then took us down to enormous high tea with the officers (the passengers get heated-up meat pie and cakes; we had salmon, roast beef and a Stilton). Then back to the wardroom to celebrate the occasion of the Captain's last voyage in command of that ship. He slipped out briefly to bring her into Wellington harbour, but returned at once, and I think we should still be in that wardroom now, singing, had not the new Captain looked in and enquired gently whether it would be all right if he sailed the ship back to Picton now.

A nicer theatre in Wellington, and show went down a treat on the first night, though again with a small audience. *Brass* is being shown out here, and the other day in Lyttelton a bus driver abandoned his bus in the middle of the street and crossed over to tell me he was enjoying it. Everyone very friendly, and they ask you in for coffee, but will they come and see the show? Not a chance.

Maidment Theatre
Auckland
December 1983

We got to New Plymouth in a howling gale – the weather changes dramatically. The Art Gallery here is said to be very fine. It was closed. We were directed to a reputedly wonderful fish restaurant. That was closed too. However, the theatre was open to those who could find it, and it is very pleasant, and in the coffee bar we met a man called Hill who had given up orthopaedic surgery to grow avocadoes, and his wife, and a poet called Elizabeth Smither. The Hills were alive to the sound of music, and said they would come and see the show; and afterwards we all went back to their avocado plantation and had a very jolly supper and stayed till the following afternoon.

Here in Auckland, Terry and I are sharing a large suite in a block of service apartments, which has a swimming pool on the roof. Today we took our towels and went up and lay in the warm sun. A number of bikini-clad nymphs wandered languidly around the edge of the pool, but without so much as a glance in our direction. I remarked on this, quietly but with perhaps a certain petulance. Terry indicated our room keys lying beside us, their large tags both displaying the same number, 19. 'That and the pink towels,' he said.

'*Super suburbia of the Southern Seas,*' (wrote Wynford Vaughan Thomas after a visit to this country some years ago),

Nature's, and Reason's, true Antipodes;
Saved by the Wowsers from the devil's tricks,
Your pubs, your shops, your minds, all close at six.

Very unfair. On the whole, we've really had a very good time. We've met some lovely, generous, hospitable people. The country, physically, is extraordinary: snow-covered Mount Cook rising out of Yorkshire-style moor-land; a bleached landscape stuck with dead gum trees on the road to that preposterous natural aberration that is Rotorua; a sandy beach at Tauronga; dark formal pine forests around the Wanganui River; tropical undergrowth with heavy palms and towering ferns, dates and lemons and big purple succulent flowers in the Bay of Islands.

Some extraordinary fauna. The *kakapo*, a nocturnal parrot, can't fly any better than the kiwi. The *tuatara* is a kind of lizard which disappeared from the rest of the world some 45 million years ago, but still has friends in New Zealand. The *peripatus* is a sort of worm with jointed limbs, and is quite disgusting to look at. All these creatures are quite rare, but then of course so are people. Particularly audiences. However, what the country lacks in human beings, it more than makes up for in sheep.

We revived Master Class *at the wonderfully
renovated Old Vic, and the show was so successful
we transferred to Wyndham's. They could only fit us
in for six weeks, as they had another show booked
in, and there was no other West End theatre vacant;
so I went back to Australia to play Churchill again –
a very unsympathetic Churchill this time – in a four-
part television film about the fall of Singapore.*

Right, that's it, the diet starts tomorrow. A delighted, very camp waiter in Macleay Street: 'It is, isn't it? I knew it was. Peter Bull!'

Rhys McConnachie excellent in *The Christian Brothers*, as is John Gaden in *The Pillars of Society* for the STC. Went to NIDA to see Nick Enright's intelligent production of Gorki's *Summerfolk*. The natural physical energy of young Australian actors, admirable though it usually is, doesn't serve them well in this instance, however. The basic behaviour that informs the play is everyone letting everyone else know that they've discovered the Secret of Life. What the NIDA students do is rush around waving their arms and shouting Hey Fellas Listen I've found the Secret of Life – whereas what perhaps they should do is gently sit next to someone and say, look, may I take up a few seconds of your time, I think this may interest you, the fact is, I've discovered the Secret of Life. Would that be funnier, or too English, maybe?

Accommodation here is palatial, though I've unaccountably been demoted from the Presidential Suite to the Hardy Amies Suite, with a dining table for six instead of fifteen, just the one gigantic fridge, only three television sets and a mere thirty-eight prints of Old Sydney. Pamela Stephenson is next door, with a very nice

113

twelve-week old daughter who will probably get to look less exactly like Billy Connolly in time. Pamela tells me she's written a revue for herself called *Naughty Night Nurses With No Knickers From Down Under Part Two*, and offered it to the Churchill Theatre, Bromley.

The filming is very hard work, very long hours, but they're a delightful unit; Chris Thompson the director is splendid, and Michael Blakemore spot-on in the central role of John Curtin. And all those great Australian heavies, Ray Barrett, Bill Hunter, Peter Whitford.

There is a quite breathtakingly attractive girl in the wardrobe department, and as she crossed the studio floor the other day, the enormous Grip (six foot three with a bare brown chest and rocks and things hanging round his neck) called out admiringly: 'Jesus, darling, if I caught the clap from you, I'd refuse treatment.' She blushed becomingly, and shimmied on. They know how to turn a compliment, these Aussies, and how to accept one.

On my return, I did two plays: The War at Home *at Hampstead, a cleverly-written play by a young American, James Duff; and a farce by Bamber Gascoigne that Pru and I were both in and both thought extremely funny, and came and went without notice at the Old Vic.*

Then I went to Switzerland to do a small part in Tender is the Night *for the BBC.*

Palace Hotel
St. Moritz
December 1984

Got here after dark, and blocking my bedroom window was a huge triangular pile of snow. In the morning, I realised I'd got the scale all wrong, that it was actually quite a large mountain quite a long way away, with a sizeable lake between us; and that the lights I'd seen twinkling at the foot of it, which I'd thought to belong to a garage and a telephone kiosk, were the lights of a distant town. The mountain, as Johnson would say, is a considerable protuberance.

When the sun comes up, church bells ring, the sky is bright blue, and the ground sparkles. People called Hans and Jurgen in anoraks clomp down the street between shops selling wristwatches, chocolate, sunglasses, little wooden models and skiing equipment. They also sell wristwatches made of chocolate, and wooden replicas of skiing equipment. Probably they sell wooden sunglasses as well, and chocolate skis made to look like wrist-watches. No cuckoo-clocks, though, I think they're all for export.

I've never seen so many expensive fur coats in my life as in one morning in St. Moritz. It offends some of the crew, who anyway feel rather out of place here, or would if it were not for DIE GROSSE BIERFESTE, held in a large hall touchingly reminiscent of the BBC Club.

Four languages are spoken here – the official one being German, but notices and menus are also printed in French. Most people speak a little English, but the staff in hotels and restaurants are nearly all Italian. They are engaged for the nine months of the tourist season, then they're all turned out of the country till it comes round again. No citizenship rights, no unemployment benefit, no sickness cover. Why hasn't Our Lady of Grantham cottoned on to this? Send the foreigners home every autumn, and they would have no national status, in spite of being allowed to spend three quarters of their annual income in the UK.

I wish I hadn't said to Rob Knights that I played tennis. He urged me to bring my racquet, which I did, and when we got up to Vulpera – a little village on the Italian border, high up in the mountains, you get out of breath just crossing the road – he booked the local in-door tennis court to play a doubles match on my first evening. He and I against two gigantic thick-set German Sparks with sweat-bands and leather thongs round their wrists. They murdered us. Rob is very good, and had had twenty-four hours to get used to the altitude, but I could hardly summon the energy to get the ball into the net, let alone over it. We abandoned it after the first set, and for some time afterwards I kept catching Rob eyeing me with bewildered concern – he couldn't believe I could have been naturally that bad – had I been playing some private anti-German joke? He didn't invite me to play again, and the subject was never referred to.

I was in the middle of a sit-com for Anglia Tele-vision when I got the news that my mother had died, suddenly. Putting things in order, arranging the funeral and so on meant an awkward series of triangular journeys between Norwich, London and Brighton where she and my father, Lockwood West, known to his fellow actors as Harry, had a cottage.

Pru, alas, was abroad at the time, doing her show about Queen Victoria.

Home
January 1985

The car wouldn't start this morning, so I decided to get the 19 bus. Have you ever done that? It's quite an event. The news that a bus is expected travels like wildfire across South London, and the tension mounts. Shops put up their shutters, schools declare a half holiday, the children prettily strew flowers in the path of the coming vehicle, and there is a band. I waited a mere three quarters of an hour at the bus stop, among a festive crowd carrying balloons and flinging streamers, and then round the corner came the triumphant bus, gleaming red, its indicator blind boldly proclaiming its intention to visit Battersea, Piccadilly Circus and Islington in the course of time. It was very exciting, and what's more, I got to Brighton in time to collect Harry and the others for the funeral.

This went very much as we could wish. The local vicar, who had actually left the parish but came back for the occasion, read a letter from Ma in answer to an article he had written in the Parish Magazine about elderly people's conception of God – it was a splendid letter, and a total surprise to Harry, who was rather moved by it. Thank you for your lovely flowers, and indeed there were a vast number of very cheering messages. The crematorium service was clinical and seemed somehow irrelevant, and we all went to the

Courtfield Hotel on the Drive for a drink or two, then back to the cottage for supper. The boys were splendid throughout. Left Harry with Patsy, then we had to come home, I feeling for the first time very empty and wishing I'd had all those conversations I'd meant to have with her. The most upsetting thing was seeing dozens of little messages dotted around the cottage – shopping lists, notes for the milkman, things to be put in the diary. It felt as if she had just gone down the road to change her library book.

I did nothing at all in the theatre this year, but
I was involved in some pretty good television – in
particular, Alan Bleasdale's four-part dramatisation
of The Monocled Mutineer, *with Paul McGann*
giving a superb performance as the anti-hero Percy
Topliss.

The Penhelig Arms
Aberdovey
Gwynedd
April, 1985

So nice to be back here at the Penhelig Arms, of all places in Wales, working, and not just visiting the Tal-y-llyn Railway.

It's lovely. Fields of daffodils, and cows ambling along in front of you, each with a tiny calf. Small black lambs butting their mothers for attention, and falling flat with the effort while the ewes graze on, regardless. And ladies in felt hats devouring scones and cream in a Lampeter tea room, criticising the sopranos in last night's Matthew Passion by the Neath Choral Society. Beautiful sunset over the Dovey Estuary, flat as a mill pond and decorated with a single fishing boat.

The hotel has been done up since we were last here, a bit prettily. Welsh dolls with knitted woollen skirts hide the spare toilet roll. A sign on my dressing table says IN CASE OF EMERGENCY AT NIGHT MRS. BREEZE CAN BE FOUND IN BEDROOM NO. 2. Mrs. Breeze is the Manageress, and a mother-substitute for all who stay there; small, grey, bespectacled, kindly and bright as a button, from the slate quarries of Caernarvon. She passes on all the gossip over a mandatory malt whisky before dinner.

Actually most of the crew are at a pub further up the coast. A few years ago the cast of *Private Schultz* stayed

122

there on location, and when the landlord found his daughter in bed with one of the actors, he turned the whole lot out into the street and said no more television people, ever. We were so short of accommodation for *Mutineer* that the BBC pleaded with him, said this was Special Projects, not like drama at all, First World War stuff, director knew Christopher Morahan, etc., etc., – and he finally yielded. Unit came up on Monday, piled into the pub; four o'clock Tuesday morning landlord finds daughter in bed with electrical rigger, RIGHT, EVERYBODY OUT, WHAT DID I TELL YOU, BLOODY BBC . . .

Can't wait to have a butcher's at the celebrated daughter. Other locals of interest include a vicar on trial for manslaughter, a psychopathic Druid in the chemist's, and a Caravan Park Hostess with pierced nipples. According to Mrs. Breeze.

Our Army Camp is in fact an abandoned RAF Training Station. Someone has bought the land and intends to turn it into a Holiday Camp (a fairly sanguine notion in this remote part of Wales, I should have thought), so he's happy for us to chop up, burn down or explode any of the buildings at will. The mutiny, when we come to shoot it, should be pretty exciting.

A lot of people inevitably are going to be offended by Bleasdale's account of the inhuman training regime at Etaples, the ensuing mutiny, and the self-structured Deserters' Community; but we have an 88-year-old ex-soldier visiting us, a captain at Etaples at the time of the mutiny, who can, and does, vouch for its accuracy.

In October, the Vatican presented an International Cultural Symposium, to mark the 1000th anniversary of the Martyrdom of St. Cyril and St. Methodias. People from all over the Catholic world were invited to take part. The Pope expressed a desire for the British contribution to be a recital of Thomas a Becket's Christmas Sermon from Murder in the Cathedral. *Probably he asked for Sir Alec Guinness to perform it, but he must have been busy and so must a number of others, because His Holiness finally finished up with me.*

The following pages were written as a diary, and sent back to Pru piecemeal.

Via di Porta San Sebastiano
Rome
October 1985

It has been arranged for me to stay with our Ambassador to the Holy See, and I was duly met at the airport by his driver, who is called Fabrizio and is young and beautiful with long black eyelashes and dark glasses on a silver chain round his neck. The house is in the S.E. corner of Rome, up a narrow side road of villas inhabited by other Ambassadors to Rome or to the Vatican. The names of their countries are displayed, with emblems, on the gateposts, rather like pub signs.

His Excellency is out, and his wife Sara just going out, to join him to sing madrigals somewhere. But she shows me the garden, very beautiful; I remark on the lovely garden wall; looks very old, I say knowledgeably. Yes, she says kindly, it is quite; 500 AD or thereabouts, it was built by Marcus Aurelius.

Because they will be out for dinner, they have fixed me to dine with Jack Buckley of the British Council. A taxi comes and I drive out past the three armed cara-binieri at the gate to a large crumbling palazzo in the city, and after twenty minutes of wandering along unin-habited marble halls and up steep echoing staircases, I find a tiny room up in the roof into which has been squeezed Jack Buckley, Susanna Walton and a grand piano. Jack takes us to a quite wonderful local restaurant, and Lady Walton tosses and gores some eminent persons of our acquaintance, very entertainingly. Took forever to get a cab to take me back to the Ambassador's villa, and when I got there the carabinieri wouldn't let me in, even though I showed them the latchkey I'd been given by the butler. They'd have to check with the Ambassador, they said. OK, I said, so check. Ambassador asleep, they said, can't wake him. I began to feel very un-keen about the whole exercise, and had just decided it was probably not too cold to sleep on a bench in the park, and was walking away to do that when they suddenly relented and let me in.

At breakfast next morning, I meet the Ambassador, David Lane, very nice, very musical, writing book on Peter Warlock. Sara used to work in the literary department of London Management. There is a cat called Paul, who was born in a doll's pram in Kingston, Jamaica. The performance is not until tomorrow, but I was supposed to be called for a rehearsal at the Vatican this morning, by Monsignor Don Lavagna, who is directing the whole entertainment; but there's been no phone call, and he doesn't answer when we ring his office at the Vatican.

So I drive into town with David to his Embassy, very compact but rather beautiful, and do some shopping, but still no word from Don Lavagna. However, when we go back home for lunch, there the gentleman is, small, agile, gold teeth, black sweater, no canonicals, very theatrical, enormous appetite. Quite a lot of other guests, including Jack Buckley and Susanna Walton, and a delicious lunch. Don Lavagna did suggest, mildly, a rehearsal in the afternoon, but was really keener on showing Susanna the Papal Gardens. He drove off after lunch in a very small Fiat, and we followed in a similar model belonging to Jack, for which he is somewhat too large. Lady W. sat beside him, and Louetta Hicks, wife of the British Council Supremo for Italy, struggled into the back with me. Jack had to reverse down the narrow lane to get out, and two things immediately became clear to us; first, that he was deeply unconfident about going backwards, and second, that the car had no handbrake. Arms rigid, eyes popping, sweat soaking his Savage Club tie, he very gently ruined the back corner of his car against Marcus Aurelius' brickwork.

Susanna was clearly used to this. 'Jack, come forward. Forward. Accelerator. Let the clutch in. No, take your foot off the brake. It's all right, you can't run backwards, you've run backwards already, that's why we're embedded in the wall. Forward, that's it. No, turn the wheel the other way – right hand down, no, *right* hand, no, down – don't take your foot off the clutch. Ah. Yes, you see we go back into the wall when you do that. Try again . . . '

Later in the day she confided to me, 'I cannot get Jack to master the art of balancing the accelerator and the clutch. If you are driving a car without a handbrake, it is the first thing you must learn – I try to tell him, but you see how nervous he gets.' I suggested that perhaps one way out of the difficulty would be to get the handbrake fixed, and this idea seemed to intrigue her.

Don Lavagna waits for us at St. Paul's gate, gives the Swiss Guard an affectionate hug, and signs us into the private City. He shows us first the Sala Nervi, where I shall be performing. Now, I had been picturing a small exquisite candle-lit chamber with a Michelangelo ceiling, a lectern, by Bernini possibly, and a small, comfortably-seated audience consisting of the Pope and a few chosen Cardinals. But no. The Sala Nervi, built in 1978, holds 8,000 seated, and can be converted to seat just 5,000 but with another 10,000 standing at the back. It is so big that the opposite end is shrouded in mist. We postpone coming to grips with this monster by going off for a ramble round the gardens.

These are very formal, though there's a charming section we only glimpsed, which is Pope Only. The City is architecturally very haphazard, old buildings jostling with unsympathetic new, but St. Peter's, which looks much more imposing from this angle, overshadows everything. Saw the railway station – just one track, with a run-round, finishing in a short tunnel at one end of the single platform, and at the other sealed off by a huge iron portcullis, which is only raised to let the very occasional train in and out. Hardly used at all now, but John XXIII liked using it, travelling in a short train of ordinary coaches to Rome Central, there to be attached to a Government train. The first time he did this, apparently, the arrangements were made in a hurry, and the honorary stationmaster, who hadn't been profession-ally called on for months, arrived from his interrupted lunch flustered and without his whistle. Having installed His Holiness and party, he begged forgiveness while he went to look for his whistle in order to dispatch the train in the traditional manner. He was rather a long time, and Pope John, worried about his connection at Rome Cen-tral, leaned out of the window, put two fingers in his mouth and whistled, and the train moved off.

Back to the Sala Nervi, where Don Lavagna robes me, to my surprise, in a sort of Am-Dram Archbishop's mitre and cope, with bits of costume jewellry stuck on with Bostik. I suppose it might look all right from a distance – distance, what am I *saying*, if they can see there's a person there, it'll be good news, let alone whether he's dressed as an Archhishop – though the mitre is about two sizes too small, and falls off when I lean forward. No ring, they've forgotten the ring, never mind. I am then led to a dressing room where there are four small altar boys in surplices, chewing gum, and I'm introduced as 'il Archivisco'. They drop to their knees and kiss my hand, puzzled by the absence of the episcopal ring. Don Lavagna shrieks with laughter, explains I'm only an actor really, and they immediately lose interest. They are to process with me across the vast stage till I reach my lectern, so we try this. There's no lectern, so I just travel a quarter of a mile or so to where it might be if we had one, and stop. An army of people suddenly appear, offering different lecterns, and different microphones to go with them. Sound system seems very good – it needs to be. Lighting also well up to professional standard.

Don Lavagna is bothered that our procession looks boring, and introduces a lot of business for me with a thurible. Looks easy when he does it; I try, hopeless, acolytes giggle. Try again, no better, Don Lavagna suggests I take thurible home with me and practice. So I put this priceless piece of Vatican History in a green plastic bag, get into Jack's Fiat, and we drive away.

Or we attempt to. As Jack winds his window down to give our names at the gate, the Swiss Guard notices the smell of incense, and espies the still-smoking thurible in the bag between my knees. He asks me to get out. I'm led into Guard Room, asked to account for my possession of this valuable artifact. Jack follows, trying to explain in broken Italian. Guard Sergeant impassive. On our suggestion he rings Don Lavagna in the Sala, and in his office; no reply from either. I think, well, Swiss Guard, probably he speaks French, so I explain, in French, that I'm a British actor rehearsing being an archbishop, and his manner changes abruptly. 'Vous êtes comedien anglais?' he asks keenly. 'Connaissez-vous Benny Hill?' I take a deep breath and lie, extravagantly, about my close intimacy with Benny Hill, whom I've never met in my life, and after a bit of a chin-wag about good old Ben, and a lot of back-slapping, he lets us go.

Tomorrow's performance was to have been at 11.00 a.m., but was this morning changed to 2.00. When I get back to the Lanes, they tell me their latest information is that it will be at 4.30, but this must not be regarded as final. This sort of thing seems perfectly acceptable to the Romans.

Next morning, did an hour's incense-swinging, making the house smell like a religious bordello, but Sara was very nice about it. Went with them to look at a church they hadn't seen, San Clemente, fifth century catacombs. They haven't been in Rome very long, so they're still enthusiastic sightseers, which is lovely for me. (Also, they don't yet know the names of some of their Diplomatic colleagues, and tend to say, 'The Norwegian was at the Post Office this morning', or 'there go the Egyptians', or 'Mrs. Spanish is coming for a drink, and possibly Mrs. Irish Number Two'.)

After lunch, back to the Vatican, but the performance time has been changed again, to 5.30, wish I'd brought a book. Don Lavagna now completely new person, terse, efficient, clip-board, headset. (But still hasn't provided a ring for me). There are already 7,000 people in the auditorium, and on stage there are 300 pilgrims, singing while the house continues to come in. The front rows fill up with Cardinals, Bishops, Monsignori, Civic dignitaries. Throne for Pope in the centre aisle. Vatican Radio, RTI, paparazzi. Backstage is Irene Papas, having a temperament about her hair, some jolly Bulgarian actors wandering around with no shirts while a distraught old lady in a mantilla irons furiously in a corridor. My altar boys sit on

130

a bench, reading comics. Some French musicians are tuning up in a courtyard, the singer who's with them chats to me about the English theatre, with particular reference to Benny Hill.

Suddenly, lots of people are running about; doors slam, security men appear with walkie-talkies, Swiss Guards come to attention. The Pope comes through from his private apartments, accompanied by a Cardinal who is head of the Propaganda Department, and his personal chaplain. Huge round of applause as he comes on stage. He sits down, and the performance starts, 6.00.

Irene Papas and a Greek group do a classical religious text, with a song at the end. Then there is a Slovenian company, who perform a long, shouted, duologue between the martyred Saints Cyril and Methodias; then it's the Bulgarians in something very similar but involving an awful lot of people jumping about, and I get dressed and the boys put away their comics and light the candles and the thurible, and we go on.

The lectern, over which we spent so much time yesterday, has been placed at the wrong height, tilted at the wrong angle, and covered with a heavy embroidered cloth so that the Bible won't stay on it. I give the thurible to the first boy, as rehearsed, and the second boy, as rehearsed, hands me the Bible that contains my text. But I have to give it back again, in order to fix the lectern. I remove the heavy cloth, and hand it to the first boy, who takes it and passes the thurible to the second boy, who delivers the Bible to the third boy, who hands on his candle to the fourth, who ends up with both candles. The laugh that this gets from the audience fills some of the twenty minutes it takes me to find and operate the various knobs which control the height and angle of the lectern – the microphone has been switched on, and every time I touch the lectern there is a sound like a gun-shot, at which the security men look round wildly.

Finally I get it fixed, the boys do another round of pass-the-parcel, and I get my Bible back. I place it on the lectern and open it at the page where my sermon has been pasted in, to find that they have closed the book before the paste was dry, and the pages are stuck together. The amplified noise of my tearing them apart is truly horrifying – thousands cover their ears, but the Pope sits bravely impassive.

They sit through it obediently, and at the end I bow, as instructed, and wait for the purposed blackout, but there isn't one, and from the wings I see Don Lavagna motioning me down stage. So I obediently come forward, His Holiness rises to greet me, we bow to each other, he says hello and thanks me for coming, in English, and thanks the altar boys and the British Diplomatic contingent who have lined up beside me, and I go off to get changed while an Italian company do a long and (according to the Lanes afterwards) spectaculary boring play about an Eighth Century miracle in Tuscany. Everyone except the British enjoy this the best, though, because they understand it. At last some Cardinals come on and talk about the two celebrated martyrs.

The Pope gets up and thanks everybody, in Italian. Then in French. Then German. Then English. Then Spanish. Finally, and extensively, in Polish. It's very impressive, but takes ages. People cough, get up and chat, call for their cars, leave the building. I thought everyone had to pay attention when the Pontiff spoke, but clearly not. By the time he finished, half his congregation were on their way home.

To dinner with nice British scientist, sit next to clever Biological Anthropologist known throughout Rome ungraciously as the Ape Girl. We go on a bit. Next morning David, in Court Dress, goes off to High Mass at St. Peter's; Sara in grey suit and hat to Anglican Harvest Festival round the corner; I get into the Daimler for the airport and home.

On my return, I started work on a TV film about the notorious Dr. John Bodkin Adams. This was produced by the late and incomparable Innes Lloyd, and filmed mainly in the Doctor's home town of Eastbourne. The long courtroom sequence, however, had to be done in Liverpool.

Liverpool is looking terribly sad. The unemployment, the under-investment, the various goings-on within the local authority, have produced a feeling of depression you can cut with a knife. It's visible in the familiar ways – uncleaned shop windows, unreplaced torn posters, uncleared litter.

We're filming in St. George's Hall, where there are two splendid traditional courtrooms, now unused. Indeed the whole place, with its magnificent ballroom, is unused; unkempt and unheated, and like to remain so. Local Government view its provisions as 'elitist' apparently. There is a fine Willis organ, that hasn't been played for years, and one lunch hour we got the organist from the Anglican Cathedral down to give it a go. It was a melancholy occasion. About twelve of us from the unit sat in a row in the vast freezing hall, our breath rising in clouds as this once splendid instrument, leathers now decayed through wilful neglect, piped the last plaintive notes that it will probably ever utter.

They're only just beginning to mess about with the decor of the Adelphi, which is still a fine building. In order tò boost trade at weekends, the place is swathed in garish posters advertising cheap deals and give-aways. Surely this is silly? If you're being given a luxury hotel experience at a cut price, you want it to look and feel like a luxury hotel, not a bucket shop. You don't want to be told every minute of the day that you're on a cheapo bargain.

On Friday night the 2,300-seater Empire was crammed to the doors for Scottish Opera's *Magic Flute*. I remember we did the same business there with the Old Vic. They operate a low seat-price structure, and the audience is drawn from every social and economic group. But the Council are selling it to a private contractor, and it will be interesting to see what happens to the programme and the prices. The Playhouse, the Everyman and the Philharmonic Hall are all, one way and another, under threat. Is the Labour Council's attitude convinced philistinism, or is it a ploy to screw more money out of the Government by penalising what they choose to think of as Tory-patronised institutions? Who are they really hurting, the people who come in on the bus, or those who can just as easily drive over to Manchester?

From time to tune, Terry Wale and I were still doing the odd single performance of Beecham *around the country, and in 1986 Michael Colgan of the Gate Theatre Dublin booked the show in for a brief season.*

Arbutus Lodge Hotel
Cork
January 1986

My first time ever in Cork. Close your ears and you might be in Italy: narrow steep winding lanes between tall stone walls protecting convents, missions, and important-looking private dwellings. I'm here for Sunday night. The man from whom I hired a car in Dublin said, 'Here's two keys, they're both the same, but one doesn't fit, so use the other one.' When I was looking for this hotel, I asked a passer-by who replied, 'No, I've no idea, I'm a stranger to Cork itself; but when you find it, I'm sure you'll have a grand evening.' And so I did.

Michael Colgan runs the Gate in masterly fashion, and it was interesting to see the Abbey, with three times the resources, announcing on Wednesday a forthcoming season of plays nearly all of which were done at the Gate last year. Saw a very good production of *Blithe Spirit* which preceded us – a definitive Madame Arcati by Rosaleen Linehan, a brilliant ageless actress. Alan Stanford splendid. Packed.

We're packed, too, which is nice, and the staff and the actors elsewhere in the city couldn't be more friendly. The stage staff all drink in a pub called, simply, 'Pauline's', which is down a dark side street beside a de-consecrated Victorian church. The narrow door is always locked, and you have to knock twice and wait for

138

Pauline to have a look at you, and if she likes you, let you in. This is not because of any dubious manipulation of licensing laws, she keeps the same hours as any other pub, it's simply her way. It's not even specially nice inside, ugly neon lighting and torn Rexine on the benches. But it is understandably fairly empty, and the clandestine nature of the operation appeals to the company's sense of the dramatic. Mind you, most of them don't drink – there are a tremendous number of tee-totallers in Dublin, they can't all be reformed alcoholics – and indeed the only person I met in Pauline's who was well into a bottle of Jameson's was the Headmaster of a Public School in Waterford, who had a thing about Winston Churchill.

Unemployment is bad here, wages low, quite a lot of begging, quite a bit of petty crime. You can't leave a car in a back street at night. Friday evening, during the show, two small boys climbed into the cab of an un-attended bus standing on the hill above the theatre, let the handbrake off and jumped out. It rolled swiftly down the hill and bellowsed five parked cars, one belonging to our DSM, the others to members of the audience. Awful, but it must have been huge fun.

We were both in Ronald Eyre's splendid production of Priestley's When We Are Married *at the Whitehall Theatre. In fact, we worked together rather a lot this year; the Priestley was televised, and we also did Joe Orton's* What the Butler Saw *together for the BBC. So, no more letters until I went to Zimbabwe to play a minor role in the film* Cry Freedom *for Richard Attenborough.*

I went out a few days beforehand to Kenya, to catch up with my son, who was touring the country with the Oxford University Dramatic Society for the British Council.

Julian Glover is here but leaving tonight, so dashing this off so that he can take it with him.

Arrived in Nairobi first thing on Thursday, and tried to trace the whereabouts of the OUDS Tour office, but nobody seemed to know. Left a message for Sam on the Message Tree, a great fat tree outside a café in the centre of Nairobi which is its unofficial Post Office. He didn't see my note, but left one for me, which I didn't see. However, at eight o'clock we met up, with great whoops, in the High Commissioner's drawing room. They'd thrown a really splendid party for the seventeen undergraduates and gave us a very good dinner. The company did bits from the various shows in the drawing room, rather well, then Mrs. High Commissioner put them all to bed somewhere.

Next morning I hired a car, and drove Sam and his friend John 200 km up to Nyere, where the company were doing *Macbeth* at a Teacher Training College. Rice and cabbage lunch, most of which the teachers threw out of the window, and then the performance – an audience of about 300. Good production, in modern battledress; the Macbeth and Macduff both chunky Australians. Sam fine as Duncan, a bit wholesome as Seyton.

The teachers' attitude was very interesting. All the witchcraft stuff, which included a lot of maltreatment of

141

dolls, got hoots of knowing laughter. Sex and violence drew from them shouts of encouragement. But they loved the language, and were quick to approve anything especially concisely and attractively put. 'I dare do all that may become a man, / Who dares do more, is none' got an appreciative and delighted laugh, and a lot of nodding. I talked to several of the teachers, they say they study only three plays of Shakespeare, and very very rarely get their students to perform. Nor do they see anything performed – many of them have never been as far as Nairobi. I think OUDS have done a really good job, and they'd held two very good workshops for the teachers, apparently, in the morning.

Sam and the others had to go on to the next date, so I drove back alone and had a blow-out on the terrible road and had to change the wheel in the pitch dark. But nothing ate me.

Got to the airport at 7.45 this morning to find, first, that the Harare flight had been delayed until 1.30, and second, that my name had been left off the flight list, even though I had rung twice to check. The flight was full, but they gave me a boarding card anyway, which seemed capricious. However, I got on.

I declared my two remaining 100 shilling (£5) notes at Customs, which you have to, and was told I couldn't take them through. Bank closed for lunch, Duty Free only take hard currency. So what do I do, I asked the officer? He beamed, took one of the notes, and put it inside his hat. 'One for you, one for me!' he explained. 'Bye bye!'

The Harare Sheraton is a bizarre looking building – all gold metal, like a giant Benson and Hedges packet, but with each part of the roof curved into a dome. The architect, I understand, was Swiss, and had built several hotels in this form, the idea of the domes being to prevent the retention of snow. It doesn't snow in Zimbabwe, ever. The place is very comfortable, except that nothing quite works. All the internal phone numbers are wrong, the plug won't stay in the bath, and most of the lamps have fused. The complimentary shampoo looks, smells and behaves like strawberry jam.

Harare Sheraton Hotel
September 1986

We finished early yesterday afternoon, so I picked up the slim pamphlet in my room entitled 'What's on in Harare', and found that the Harare Playhouse was presenting Roger Hume in *Old Herbaceous* – the solo piece about an old gardener written, I think, by Alfred Shaughnessy and first produced at Salisbury (UK). So I went along. Lots of middle-aged ladies in hats – the only black face in the building was behind the coffee counter. Charming performance, and a perfect audience for it. Before it started, a lady sitting next to me got chatting about England, and how she was so worried about Robert Mugabe that she was strongly tempted to move back to Gloucestershire, which she'd left when she was three. 'But,' she complained, 'I gather it's almost impossible to get good staff, and people to do your gardens.' (I'm not lying about the plural.) She told me she taught in a private girls' school in Harare, and assumed she could pick up something similar in England. I had to tell her I thought that was almost as doubtful as getting all those people to do her gardens, and she clicked her teeth and said she hadn't quite realised things were as bad as that at home. 'Nothing a change of Government wouldn't sort out', I said cheerily. In the interval she moved to another seat.

I'm fond of the Zimbabweans, whose outlook (in marked contrast to that of the Kenyans) appears to me generally optimistic and benign. Mugabe seems to spend money on the right things – health, education, roads, agricultural development. They're remarkably tolerant of the White Rhodies, who sometimes behave appallingly, and at the same time work very happily alongside Europeans who are prepared to embrace the system. And I've met a lot of South African Europeans who can't cope with their own regime any more – engineers, farmers, architects – and have come over the border to work for considerably less money and in far less luxurious conditions. There's a very good feel about the place.

I'm snatching a weekend at Victoria Falls before I come back, crummy old tourist that I am.

*In early 1987 we rehearsed a television play for the
BBC,* Harry's Kingdom, *to be shot on film in outer
London. A TV electricians' strike threatened not to
have resolved itself by the time we were due to start
filming; however, the BBC electricians in Northern
Ireland were* not *on strike, so an emergency plan
was formed to shoot the whole thing north of Belfast
if necessary. The Director and Designer went over to
look at locations, and we rehearsed every scene in
two separate set plans, depending on where we
finally were to end up. As things turned out, it was
Belfast.*

Co. Antrim
N. Ireland
February 1987

Um, yes, glad you liked the Valentine . . . very glad . . .
the only thing, um, is, that, well, in a way, er, I didn't,
personally speaking, actually send it, so

WHO WAS IT FROM?

I mean, I *did* get you one, and it's still in my brief
case, because I forgot to post it. But thank you for – um
– yours?

I'm liking Robert Young extremely, very enjoyable to
work with; the only trouble is he keeps thinking of
lovely extra details to put in, and we go wildly overtime
every day. Hope they can borrow of the night a dark
hour or twain when it comes to transmission. The
budget must be extraordinary.

It all looks very right, and the extras here are
wonderful – a lot of them fully-fledged professional
actors doing us a favour. It's a shame we'll have to re-
voice a lot of the general chat to take out the Belfast
sound, because their improvised double-glazing-salesmen
dialogue is masterly and hilarious.

A letter came yesterday, forwarded, from Esmond
Knight, saying he'd heard the radio programme I did
about Norman Douglas. Very funny letter. He told me
that when he was a small boy, he and a school friend
were accosted in the Natural History Museum by a florid

146

man in a tweed suit who put his hand up their trouser legs and who subsequently turned out to be Norman Douglas. I was actually writing a reply to Esmond when out of the corner of my eye I caught sight of his *obituary*, in the paper – he'd died, the day after he wrote the letter. It was an awful, almost obscene shock.

This pub is very pleasant, but right out in the country, so we're stuck in the evening unless we share a cab to go into Belfast. There's a great deal more soldiery about now, and festoons of barbed wire in places I hadn't noticed it before. Some of the more politically earnest members of the cast try to strike up conversations in bars about the Situation, but nobody really wants to talk about it – it's far too complicated, there can be no equable solution, people don't trust the politicians on either side; and to all but a relative few, life depends on pretending it's still the same lively, open-hearted city it's essentially always been.

I'd been doing a play by Brian Phelan, The Signalman's Apprentice, *at Southampton, and it was hoped to produce it in London. However, problems arose as they so often do, and nothing happened. So no theatre again in 1987. Instead, I spent two months growing a beard and learning Spanish for the leading part in a Basque film,* Balanza. *Unfortunately, the new Film Finance Director in Madrid didn't like the Basques, and withdrew the Government funding; so the film was postponed for a year, by which time they'd thought of somebody else. Somebody Spanish, perhaps.*

Anyway, I went off to Vienna to be in an Italian Television film called The Sealed Train, *starring Ben Kingsley as Lenin.*

Hilton International
Vienna
June 1987

Well, I went to the Kammerspiele last night to see *Was der Butler Sah,* and on the whole I don't think we need to worry about our own BBC production. It seemed to me they didn't understand the style at all, cut some of the best lines (my German is just good enough to understand what isn't being said), and put in loads of extraneous comic business. The director was Cyril Frankel, for whom I did a 'Randall and Hopkirk' at Elstree the year Joe was born. A potentially wonderful actor playing Prentice. He looked like Cecil Parker in pebble glasses, and should have been playing Rance. The Rance was thin and nervous and of course should have been playing Prentice; later, I met an actress from the Kammerspiele and asked her about this – she explained that the older actor was the senior member of the company, and therefore had to play the largest part. What about when they do *Romeo and Juliet,* I wondered. The rest of the cast not impressive, and the middle-aged burghers and their wives sat and sucked their breath through clenched teeth.

This is the first taste I have had of Viennese theatre since that four-hour prose version of *Antony and Cleopatra* we saw at the Burgtheater in 1969, where nobody in the cast was under the age of forty-five and the

149

set consisted of about a hundred and thirty copper sheets whanging in and out. There's a lot going on just now though, as it's Festival time, so I must keep trying. There's a new Edward Albee at the English Speaking Theatre, which is advertised as having been directed by Albee himself, though people stoutly maintain Kevin Billington did it. I'll go, anyway.

Quite hard to find good music, too. Plenty of Johann Strauss, and about eight different productions of *White Horse Inn* going on simultaneously. They name streets after Mozart, Schubert, Brahms, Beethoven, Haydn, Bruckner, but don't seem to play any of their music. Georges Pretre is coming to the Musikverein, but not till after I've gone. The Head Porter here has got me into the Domingo *Otello* tomorrow night, though, for about a fifth of what it would cost me at Covent Garden. And there was a street concert this morning in honour of NATIONAL MILCHWOCHE, given by a brass band of milkmen in grey suits and Tyrolean hats, and they were superb.

One thing I love about Vienna is the pedestrian subways. The kind of underpass that in Britain is normally dark, filthy, dangerous and smells of pee, here in Vienna will be attractively lit and scrupulously clean. There will be little shops and a coffee bar, musicians will be playing, and there might be a children's art exhibition on the walls. On the other hand, jay-walking across the road above attracts fierce penalties, which is fair enough if there's a viable alternative.

I'm enjoying the filming. Damiano Damiani is lovely, very funny and intelligent, and lets me say whatever I like in my scenes, an attitude I always find endearing in directors. But the First Assistant is the real eminence grise of the outfit: he's called Enrico Bergier, has perfect English and German which Damiano doesn't, and shouts at him a lot though they're obviously fast friends. It's quite difficult to ascertain the nationalities of some of the crew, who tend to have names like GOLLY MARBOE, LUCKY ENGLANDER, ALFRED BLOBSACK and PLATON KUCHAL DE WILD. Fellini's make-up man, Manlio Rocchetti, adds hairs to my feeble Spanish beard with latex, which takes hours, and then tongs them. Looks wonderful. At the end of the day, he takes it all off by shaking a can of lighter fuel over my face, smoking fiercely the while, and then plucking me like a chicken.

Hope the thing is going to be *interesting* enough. So much of the story is simply about whether the sealed train will get Lenin back to Russia. Well, we know that it did, don't we, so what we're left with is a lot of incidental personal relationships that develop en route, and this is rather tame, even with the sudden introduction of Lesley Caron. There again, when you're on a train you're terribly limited as to shots, all of which must be only too familiar to the viewer. Ben uses those famous piercing brown eyes in close-up as much as he reasonably can, but there are limits.

Of course, I love the train itself. They haven't let me drive the locomotive yet, or even fire it, but I'm hoping.

In 1987, Granada produced a dramatised reconstruction of the previous year's Reagan-Gorbachev Arms Talks, for which I assumed the famous birthmark.

Then, for the BBC, Strife, *Galsworthy's drama about the conflict of industrial interests between shareholders and workforce, which suddenly seemed alarmingly up-to-date. We shot a great deal of it at Blist's Hill, Ironbridge, in the few murky hours of December daylight.*

Quite an abrupt change, then, to find myself in Kenya the following month, to play Stefanie Powers' father in A Shadow on the Sun, *for CBS Television.*

Aberdare Country Club
Nyere
Kenya
January 1988

Claire Bloom, Nicola Pagett, Freddie Treves, Trevor Eve, Brian Cox, Joe Mydell and I are up here in the Aberdare mountains, and having a great time.

We've seen quite a lot of game – too much, the African guides say. They're very worried by how the animals have come to accept humans as part of the landscape – they even appear to pose for photographs. The other day we were out on a drive and one of those gazelles or dykdyks or whatever they are ran out in front of us, hotly pursued by an adult leopard. When the leopard saw us, it stopped, looked at us, and lay down to be photographed, while the gazelle, which I suppose should properly have been its lunch, disappeared into the bush. That's no way to be a leopard, it seems to me.

We've also seen a bongo, which is accounted quite something to brag about.

A Shadow on the Sun is the tale of Beryl Markham – racehorse-trainer, aviatrix, society adventuress and, in her later years, hopeless lush. As a story, it has everything, and brings in as a bonus all the familiar characters of Kenyan scandal. Tony Richardson is directing it beautifully, but has difficulty seeing eye-to-eye with the producers, and occasionally with the star. Stefanie has to

153

go from about seventeen to eighty-three, tough for any actress, and any cameraman. I have a slightly easier time – around twenty-eight at the beginning (but never in close-up), and I peg out at about seventy.

Beryl's head groom is played by Joe Mydell, a very good young black American actor who is resident in the UK. His father is played by a stunning-looking Masai called Fred Owalu. The other day I watched him, six foot six inches tall and in full war paint, being shown by a small bespectacled man in a safari suit how to throw a spear. A solicitor in Nairobi, Fred has never handled such a thing in his life, and indeed is rather nervous of it.

We have been filming on a farm owned by a very charming Anglo-Kenyan lady, and yesterday while they were setting up a shot, she asked the actors into her drawing-room for tea. There was something uneasy in her manner, and I suddenly realised that she didn't quite know what to do about Joe being in the room. Of course she was aware he wasn't an African, she knew perfectly well he was a highly-educated American, but nevertheless, he was black, and she was flummoxed. She couldn't ask him to pass round the tea cups, but on the other hand, she couldn't bring herself to ask him to sit down. On her sofa. Joe sat down anyway, I'm glad to say, and after a while she stopped fidgeting, but it was very noticeable, and quite disturbing.

In general, Anglo-Kenyan Society has been good to us. Everyone knows everyone else, and of course I've met a lot of friends of your brother Tim, and and of Kathryn's family. These are mostly the people who *do* things, they're farmers, or engineers, or vets, or they're involved in some way in big game tourist industry. But there are an awful lot of people who *don't* do much, except play polo or breed Pekingese or go show-jumping. A lot of young people fall into this category, and I find that rather depressing. Parents send their offspring away to school in England or Scotland, and then they come back to Kenya. The boys, I suppose, find jobs, most of them, but it seems the girls are just waiting around to get married, filling up the interval by going to each other's gymkhanas. 'I'm taking Mags over to Buffy's,' I heard one of them say this morning. Then again, it might have been Buffy, over to Mags'.

Jack Thompson, the Australian star, has just joined us, and is terrific. He can fix everything – a recalcitrant horse, a car that won't start, the pump from the well I'm supposed to have dug, which defeated the props department – 'Gimme a spanner,' says Jack, and fixes it. He's living down the hill in Nyere with most of the unit, and they're paralytic every night.

Do you know the kind of Second Assistant who believes that what you need when you arrive at the location at 6.00 a.m. is loud, cheery banter? The kind that wears khaki Bermuda shorts, smells slightly of sour milk, and calls you Squire. (Well, I don't know what he calls the girls.) Anyway, we've got one here. Trevor Eve, James Fox and I are throwing dice to see which of us is to kill him.

We filmed David Storey's fine play The Contractor *at Skipton, West Yorkshire. This was the last of several plays I did with Barry Davis, a splendid director who died tragically shortly afterwards. It was also, for me, the end of*Theatre Night, *a selection of plays written for the theatre, but reproduced using television techniques rather than emphasising their theatrical origin. The series, under the aegis of Shaun Sutton, was admirable, and I was proud to be a member of what we used to call the Sutton Rep.*

The BBC, however, decided not to continue the idea, and my next job for them was in something designed more for the general market – Campion. *The Wonder Horse.*

Church End
Broxted
Essex
July 1988

I've escaped from The Moat House to somewhere cheaper and more luxurious.

Note that *A Shadow on the Sun* has made it to the cover of the TV Times. 'Her Life with the Wild World of Africa', runs the legend, under a cobbled-together picture of Stefanie Powers with two tiger cubs. Full marks to the Picture Editor for selecting about the only feline creature not to be found anywhere on the African continent.

And a consolation prize to the Birmingham Mail – a clipping arrived from the agency with a notice for *Strife*. Above the caption 'Timothy West as Hard Union Chief' is a picture of me as Mikhail Gorbachev, complete with birthmark.

By the way, did I tell you about wandering out on to the Granada Tours building site when I was playing Gorbachev? I wanted to have a look, so I slipped out in the lunch-hour, in full costume and make-up, through the back door. A man in a hard hat challenged me. 'Do you work here?' he demanded. 'No,' I told him, 'I am General Secretary of the United Soviet Socialist Republics.' 'Well,' he said, 'you'll have to ask at the main gate.'

This is a very leisurely production, everyone very unrufflable, but my feeling is it could be going a lot quicker. Carol Gillies and I sit out on the lawn for hours, chat and do the crossword. Of course the house is fiendishly difficult to shoot in, all dark corners and twists and bends – it looks as if it's going to be perfect for a whodunnit, until you come to work in it.

Mary Morris is playing my mother. Very few people play my mother any more, I find, but I suppose Mary is over eighty. She is phenomenal. Built her own house in the Swiss Alps, and still drives a battered Land Rover. Last night, when we'd wrapped, I saw her hunting in the grass for something. She told me it was one of her brass costume earrings, that had dropped off as she was on her way to the make-up caravan. We searched together for a while, without success; then, as the sun had gone down and it was getting chilly and her car was waiting, I suggested we gave it up as a bad job. She agreed, very reluctantly. The next morning, on the set, I noticed she was wearing both the earrings. 'Oh,' I said, 'so you found it?' 'No,' she replied, 'I made a replacement last night. Does it look all right?' Somehow she'd got hold of a strip of brass, some wire, a soldering iron and some tin-snips, and *made* this earring in her hotel bedroom. I'm speechless.

Michael Frayn translated three of Chekhov's one-act plays, and dramatised some of his short stories, under the title of The Sneeze, *and we did it for Michael Codron at the Aldwych. Ron Eyre had cast Rowan Atkinson, Cheryl Campbell and me in the leading roles, and I think believed that the mixture would produce rather an exciting confection. Actually our styles are so dissimilar that it didn't, really; and Rowan's audience, though he was wonderfully funny, hadn't really come to see Chekhov.*

The cast seemed to be terribly accident-prone, and due to emergency understudy rehearsals I had to cancel what would, as it turned out, have been my last visit to my father. He'd been ill, and died fairly suddenly on the 28th of March.

The death of your surviving parent moves you up a generation overnight. While you have a mother or father living, you feel you are in a sense still growing, that there's more to come. With their death you have to recognise that this is it, you've grown up, this is how you'll be from now on. It's perhaps a harder lesson for actors than for other people.

Anyway, when The Sneeze *came off, I took another of my sideways steps. I had been doing a certain amount of work for the International Foundation for Training in the Arts. They had a scheme to send sixteen students from eight of the top Drama Schools in the UK to study for a month at the Moscow Art Theatre School, and I agreed to rehearse, accompany and generally look after them. I already*

159

knew Oleg Tabakov, The Principal of the School; also Oleg Gerasimov, the Dean, who had stayed with us when his students had been invited over by the RSC.

So we left on 9th April, 1989, and again I kept a diary, which I posted home in instalments.

Orlyonok Hotel
Moscow
April 1989

The plane was a very old Ilyushin, quite noisy, with a very high roof and varnished wood everywhere; rather charming. ('By some Ilyushin see thou bring her here': M.N.D., III 2). Lunch not too bad, some passable red plonk, good coffee.

On board, met a party of British lawyers, on the way to study the Russian legal system. One of them, Eric Crowther, was actually at school with me. He is Stipendary Magistrate at Horseferry Road, and told me that a few days ago a man had been up before him for stealing a designer T-shirt from Harrods, priced, incredibly, at £141. Crowther inspected it, astonished, and said: 'I would never give £141 for a T-shirt!' 'Just what I felt, your honour,' came the voice from the dock.

We all drank vodka out of paper cups and had a very jolly time.

Our party got through customs at Moscow very easily, but then we were told by our interpreters that our bus had broken down, and wouldn't it be nice if we waited another hour for the BA flight so that we could share a bus with some students from Leicester University, as we're all going to the same place? There is a big international student drama festival called PODIUM going on in Moscow, and it is impossible to get anybody to understand that we're not part of it. I start trying to explain the difference between University Drama Societies and Accredited Drama Schools, but the distinction rapidly begins to sound frivolous and pedantic, so I shut up. But no, thanks all the same, we're *not* going to the same place, and we *would* like our own bus.

The Orlyonok is on the South-Western outskirts of the city, and is just like any other second-class Eastern European hotel. There were the usual British Council Tour type problems of not enough rooms having been booked, people being asked to double up, passports being taken away, no facilities for changing money, nothing to eat. It was 11 p.m. Moscow time, and nowhere in the area was open. But John Woods, who is with us to make a film of it all, and who had arrived on Friday, had managed to get together a lot of cold sausage and bread and white wine, and laid it all out in Caroline's room (Caroline Keeley and I, unlike the students, get a big room each), and the whole party set to with a ferocious will.

While we're eating, the first teaching schedules arrive. Immediately there is a problem. We knew that we were to join forces with twenty-four American students from the Julliard School and elsewhere, and all our planning has assumed that the aggregate was to be divided into four groups. Now we find that Oleg Tabakov has had to take over a part in the main theatre at short notice, and will not be available to teach. Three groups only, then; Gerasimov will take one group, and the other two Professors are called Kulyagin and Bogomolov. Also, the teaching hours, according to the schedule, are absurdly short – there's a lot in the itinerary about visiting museums and people's tombs and student productions, but not much *work.*

Up next morning at 8.30, but found there was no breakfast, as the buffet had run out of food and wouldn't open again till twelve. Someone from one of the TV channels was supposed to arrive with a crew to interview me at ten o'clock, but didn't materialise. Someone else was supposed to come with our passports and roubles, but no. This, I was soon to understand, was a typical start to a typical day in Moscow, and after a while I stopped expecting anything else.

The Americans were arriving this morning, and being brought direct from the airport, so it was just Caroline and me and the sixteen students in the bus to the Moscow Art Theatre. Outer Moscow very drab and sad and undernourished-looking, but the 18th and 19th century buildings that remain are lovely, and as you get to the heart of the city and see the huge gold domes of St. Ivan the Great, the vast Stalin 1920's skyscrapers, the striped minarets of St. Basil's, it is quite magical. The city very busy, a great many cars, no advertisements of course, shop windows sadly empty – maybe just a display of toothpaste tubes, or plastic watering cans, or a single nylon jacket. A lot of queuing.

Gerasimov embraced me warmly, and asked after the family. He still chain-smokes those yellowish cigarettes that smell of apples. Our students were shown into Tabakov's study, where we waited quite a long time for the Americans to arrive. They had, however, been driven somewhere else by mistake, so Tabakov opened the proceedings with vodka, and cheese, and charm, and charisma, and wondrous stories; and when the completely enchanted students left to meet their professors, we got down to attempting to evolve a programme that could neither be said to waste the student's time nor the sponsors' money. Tabakov had just returned from a fortnight's holiday in Florida, and was much inclined to make light of the various problems I could see looming ahead.

However, we did agree that the teaching hours should be considerably augmented as soon as PODIUM, which his department had to host, was over, and at 3. 30 we went to lunch at the Actors' House, the Union building which houses libraries, performance areas, workrooms and a large and popular restaurant (three courses for one rouble eighty-five kopeks. Officially this is 1.85p, but nobody's much concerned with official rates of exchange.)

In the evening, I'm afraid I decided not to attend a performance of Ostrovsky sketches in the Art Theatre Studio, but went instead to talk to John Woods at his hotel, the gigantic Rossya, and had some dinner in the basement restaurant there. Waitress spoke some English, said there was red caviar on the menu, but, lowering her voice, 'I think you will be more comfortable with black caviar.' We said by all means let us be comfortable, and she replied, 'My friend can arrange it.' Her friend, a stony-faced waiter, came up with a couple of ounces of black caviar, still in the tin, and slipped it unobtrusively on to the table. 'Will you put ten dollars in a napkin and leave it in the gentlemen's toilet,' he hissed, and was gone. John duly obliged, noticing the waiter standing furtively in the corridor, examining the light fittings. All this cloak and dagger stuff seemed to me totally unnecessary, since everyone appears to deal quite openly in hard currency; I think they just read too many John le Carré novels. When we got outside and it was raining, we couldn't prevail upon a taxi driver to take us back to the Orlyonok until we'd promised him dollars. (We were later told off by the British Council for doing this – Marlborough cigarettes, they said, would usually produce the required result, or, in some cases, condoms. This last suggestion proved uncongenial to our female students as being open to misconstruction.)

The next day was the first day of classes. Queued for half an hour for breakfast of cheese and coffee, then went outside to solve the problem of buses. We were promised a 60-seater bus to take the whole British and American contingent to the cemetery at Novodiviche, there to pay homage, as is customary, to Chekhov and Stanislavski. But in fact there are no 60-seater buses in Russia, so we were given two smaller buses; one for us and some of the Americans, the other for the remaining Americans plus a number of Scandinavian, Israeli and Dutch participants in PODIUM, all of whom wanted to go to different places, and most of whom had to be got out of bed.

The cemetery is like a tiny model of Pere LaChaise, but not as ponderous or gloomy. Tabakov arrived, said a few words, and we laid flowers on Chekhov's tomb – he is buried between his father and sister Olga. Tabakov showed us another grave nearby, and said simply, 'Very famous actor.' I'm afraid I've forgotten his name. I asked which parts he famously played, and was told, 'Yepikhodov and Fedotik were his great roles.' My first thought was, how wonderful to have a system where someone whose best parts were on that modest level is accorded such distinction and a place in this very exclusive burial ground. My second thought, of which I am deeply ashamed, was, 'I wonder whether he became such a popular and long-standing member of the company that gradually those roles took on the appearance of very showy little cameos?' For it is undoubtedly true of the Moscow Art Company that people who are with it for life have their own quite considerable claques in the audience, and can't always resist playing to them. Not what Stanislavski was after.

We visited his grave too, of course, and that of Nemirovich-Danchenko, and Maxim Gorky, and others. The students were much affected by the visit, and so was I.

On to the School. Not enough rooms, we find; not enough interpreters; Sasha Kulyagin, the ace tutor of the three, has not turned up. A movement class is improvised, somehow we get through the morning, and the students, at lunch time, are radiant. Caroline and the American Course Director and I have a meeting with Tabakov to discuss how things should go from now on. He is exhausted, and no wonder, for as well as running a Theatre School and a Studio Theatre, rehearsing Gaev without warning and planning a new production of his own, he concerns himself personally with ordering buses, passes and tickets for us lot. He has a perfectly efficient staff, it seems to me, why can't he delegate. Only later I got the message that in Russia at present, getting things to happen depends very much on the status of who's talking down the phone. Oleg Tabakov is a nationally respected figure, and what he says goes. Well, not always, as we've seen.

Changed some money through a friend of John's, who gives ten roubles to the pound, and nine to the dollar, and is delighted to do so for everyone.

I still had the stitches from cracking my head open in Brighton, and went to the doctor at the British Embassy to have them taken out. Quite a pang when I opened the front door and found a heavy oak table with copies of Country Life and the Sunday Times, a handsome grandfather clock ticking gravely away, and a tall Sheffield ex-policeman sitting by a crackling fire. He took me across the courtyard to see a very jolly elderly doctor who had seen *Single Spies* in London last week (a must, I suppose, for all Diplomatic personnel, especially on this particular posting).

Even the nurse did a reduction for Sterling. I mean, for taking the stitches out.

Got back to the Orlyonok by the wonderful metro (I went back later to photograph many of the stations) and a trolleybus, to do some work before we all went to *Uncle Vanya* tonight; but of course we had been told the wrong starting time, and when I arrived at the hotel, the bus was waiting to take us back into town.

A very moving, but scenically absurdly elaborate production by Ephraimov, played *terribly* quietly – I wondered if those at the back could hear it at all, but perhaps they know the play by heart. A fine Vanya by Smoktunovsky, a lovely Sonya; that tall popular blonde lady we met at Balliol playing Yelyena, very actressy; and a vulgar but clearly much loved Waffles (bet he gets a place in the cemetery). Ephraimov himself playing Astrov – excellent first two acts, then he appears in the map scene in immaculate tail coat, beautifully coiffed and minus his moustache. The scene is played as high stylistic comedy, and doesn't sit at all well with the rest of the production.

Afterwards, Kevin, the American Course Director, his Administrator and I were terribly hungry. We went to the Actors' House and were told the restaurant was shut, so we trailed round Moscow scattering dollars and Marlborough cigarettes to no avail, and finally returned to the Actors' House at 12.30 a.m. to find all our students just finishing a four-course meal, with champanski.

Up to now it's always been the Americans who had to be levered out of bed to get on the bus in the morning, but the day after *Uncle Vanya* we had some British casualties as well. Indeed, a couple of them would have missed the bus altogether had it left when it was supposed to; but for a long time we couldn't find the driver, who was sitting in a remote part of the hotel waiting to be recognised, though as he was not our regular driver and no one had seen him before, this was not sensible. When we did find him, he revealed that he'd been instructed to drive us somewhere quite different, and wouldn't agree to change his destination until an order to that effect had been typed and signed by the Transport Office. This office was a considerable distance beyond the school, so he finally agreed to drop us at the school while he went on to the Transport Department to get authorisation for having driven us to the school in the first place. (It all turned out, of course, to be PODIUM's fault. I view PODIUM with odium.)

So everyone naturally was late for class. Caroline I think will have a nervous breakdown if this goes on, but it *will* go on. I've already begun to grasp that there are a few things you *can* change, others will change on their own and at their own pace, and others won't change at all, so there's no point in worrying.

A splendid talk by Prof. Anatoly Smelyansky, major dramatic critic and official historian of the Moscow Art Theatre, through an excellent interpreter of his own; and I had lunch with them afterwards. This business of booking interpreters is a further problem – we have one splendid one, Eugene, who has to be shared around all the groups because he is wildly better than any of the others, who often do not even turn up. At a prolonged meeting about this and other things, John Woods revealed that his footage of the students at Novodevichiy was ruined in the labs, also that he has asked permission to film the students visiting the Kremlin. This permission has to be granted by two different departments: one has given it for Wednesday, the other for Friday. Useless.

To the Bolshoi for *Boris Gudonov*, and met Eric Crowther and the legal gang in high spirits on the front steps, haggling with the ticket touts. The production might have been in the repertoire since before the Revolution, I think, rather a lot of royal plum velvet everywhere; but in the main wonderfully sung. Splendid bass, Morosov, was Boris, and there was a fine tenor. Chorus superb musically, though there was a lot of Worried Boyar acting and the Lithuanian Peasantry Comic Relief Scene was beyond belief; but Morosov is a terrific actor, and treated us to an amazing fall down a flight of steps and immediately carried on singing. I'd like to see *that* at Covent Garden. Fine orchestra, conducted passionately without a score by a bespectacled person of about twelve.

There were a lot of people from our National Youth Theatre there, in Moscow for PODIUM. Their President, Prince Edward, was here for a day or two, but has flown back to attend the first night of *Aspects of Love*, thus cutting an official dinner to have been held in his honour. Not a diplomatic move, people are not pleased. We had some supper with the NYT company, a very bright lot, and then went to watch the rather eerie ceremony of the midnight changing of the guard at Lenin's tomb.

I've been dodging between classes – Gerasimov, tired, cynical, funny – Kulyagin, warm, appreciative, energetic, a fine actor; and Bogomolov, elderly, crusty, pedagogic – and watching the faces of the students as they react to the different personalities. Kulyagin inspires actual love, from both sexes; Gerasimov encourages motherly care

169

from his American female students, they bring him little gifts of ham and chocolate, which he takes home to his wife, Nelly. Bogomolov scares them, but they're intrigued to know more.

We saw Tabakov's student production of *The Sailor's Return,* a play by a dissident Jewish writer that has been on his desk for 31 years, and which he has only just now been allowed to do. Fine production, and the students are a wonderful exemplification of the School's ideology. There was not a bad habit, nor a piece of untruthful or telegraphed or exaggerated acting, anywhere to be seen. They're all in their twenties, but the characters in the play were mainly people in their forties, fifties and sixties, and the performances were totally acceptable in visual appearance, movement, stance, voice, and attitude.

Moscow Art Theatre School
April 1989

Went to the Russian students' dance demonstration at lunch time – brilliant, wonderfully funny and extremely accomplished in all sorts of styles. The beautiful girls *look* like dancers, whereas when they're acting they look like ordinary people. In the canteen, they look like actresses.

Giselle at the Bolshoi this evening, rather predictable, classic choreography, fine dancing, lovely corps work, dreary sets and lighting, all the men very butch, all the girls very fragile. Then went back to supper with our favourite interpreter Eugene. He lives in a tower block some way out of the city, in one room about half the size of our kitchen, together with his young wife Lyuba and little boy Maxim. Maxim actually sleeps in a communal dormitory downstairs. Eugene is a Ph.D. language professor, and went to teach English in Delhi just after Maxim was born, because they needed the money. On his return he found that his residency permit had been withdrawn – no special reason – and the only way they can continue to live in Moscow is for Lyuba to go to the University and take a Ph.D. herself. They can continue in their room in this student block until she takes her Doctorate, but after that they will have to move out of Moscow unless some bureaucratic miracle intervenes. They are an extraordinarily well-read couple, and may well end up sweeping crossings in Nizhny Novgorod.

This student apartment block makes Keele University look like Chatsworth. Carving my way through the snow, I crossed a courtyard and entered a concrete hallway lit by a single neon strip. Among the puddles on the floor, students sat on old car seats watching a flickering black-and-white television screen. I crossed to the stairs, and as I started up them, a very tall ferociously bearded young man in a track suit and sneakers detached himself from the others, and started to follow me. I climbed a little faster. So did he. I knew I had three more floors to climb (Eugene had told me the lift didn't work), and my pursuer was gaining on me. Eventually I stopped, hoping perhaps he might pass me and carry on up, but as he drew level with me, he put out a huge hand and caught my arm. Right, I thought, this is it. All my money, my watch, my passport, perhaps my shoes.

'You English?' he asked. I admitted I was. 'I English student; here, University,' he said. He sat on the concrete step, and drew me down beside him. 'Tell me of Yeats', he demanded. 'Also Eliot.'

My lecture didn't last very long, and I went on up to Eugene's apartment, where we were given a wonderful meal of carp and cucumber and garlic and egg salad, and then steak, with five different kinds of vodka. There were about ten of us, and we all sat on the floor, and it was a lovely evening. I gather that it may have meant beans and potatoes for the family for the rest of the week.

The following night, the NYT gave their first performance of *Murder in the Cathedral*, at the Moscow Art Theatre no less, and their Council were there in force, including Prince Edward (who has flown back again for the occasion, so he's been in some measure forgiven), Illtyd Harrington and Sir David Orr. A very lavish production, music (lots of it) by Geoffrey Burgon, splendidly staged, but alas, the verse not handled at all well or securely by the young company whose usual sort of thing this isn't. HRH went back to the Rossya with the company afterwards, and had an extensive bop with the girls, which was pretty engaging.

Everything is going wrong with poor John's filming. He keeps trying to set up interviews to shoot, and either the people don't show up or he gets turned out of the location he's chosen. However, he did get to film us going round the Kremlin one afternoon. The churches are wonderful – I wish I knew more about the ikons, but the frescoes are quite clear and simple and beautiful. Packed with Russian visitors – the official rule still limits each city to one practising church, but unofficially I think the situation is easing a little. John is extraordinary with his Russian film crew, waving his hands a lot and speaking in English very loudly without prepositions or verb-endings. They just smile and get on.

Brian Cox, when he was over here, directed the Moscow Art students in *The Crucible*, and it's still in their repertoire. We went to a performance, very good production, excellently played. The last twenty minutes were completely ruined, though, by someone drilling through a neighbouring wall. Nobody, apparently, was empowered to stop it. Just like Broadcasting House.

A goodbye party for PODIUM. When I got there, all the drink had gone, there were about twelve bridge rolls and three hundred bellowing people, one of whom presented me with a frightful doll. I nipped out early with a couple of our Americans, and got a lift back to the hotel for a fountain pen and 20 Silk Cut. I then got trapped in the elevator. Eight people, all in thick overcoats.

I've often rehearsed this scene in my mind. There's a beautiful girl who's frightened and has to be calmed (by me). A man gives way to panic and has to be brought sharply to order (by me). I tell a lot of stories to maintain the morale, while keeping the company as still as possible to conserve oxygen; and I finally perceive an ingenious way of manually operating the lift to a position of safety. But I've always rehearsed it in English, with an imaginary English cast. In the actual Russian production, I had a very small part. And there was no panic at all, my fellow passengers were obviously quite accustomed to such mishaps, and laughed and joked quite happily for the twenty minutes until we were winched to the next floor.

The next morning I noticed a morose looking child hanging about the hotel corridor, so I ducked back into my room, picked up last night' s hideous doll, and thrust it into her arms. She immediately started to scream, but I bounded down the stairs before her cries could summon a parent.

Sasha Kulyagin is ill, so today his students went swimming and then to a Sauna, where it seems they were beaten with quite large trees by lusty middle-aged ladies in black one-piece bathing suits. For the male students, this was probably a relaxing change after the attentions of the female PODIUM delegates from the Akademy of Copenhagen.

The general feeling seems to be that the Americans are absorbing the teaching noticeably more slowly than our own people. This is of course partly because ours had learnt and rehearsed all their scenes for a week before we came out, whereas the Americans, through some breakdown of communications, didn't. But there's more to it than that. There's still a lot of Lee Strasberg around in American teaching – not so much from the Julliard students, but many of the others. Each has been taught to think of himself or herself as a particular kind of actor, to be cast in the way their own individual personality most easily suggests. Now this may be fine when you're doing Sam Shepard, but it doesn't stand you in very good stead for Chekhov and Ostrovsky. To the Method-educated, you're either a straight actor or a character actor, and being a straight actor is best, by a long chalk.

Now to Stanislavski, all acting is character acting, isn't it, and the Method, which claims to draw its inspiration directly from him, has misunderstood this fundamental truth.

So for instance the young Californians have terrible difficulty in forgetting their modern selves enough to make room for a few basic thoughts about where they live, what sort of schooling they've had, what they might be wearing, how far they've ridden today and how long is it since they last saw this other person, in the Ukraine, exactly a hundred years ago. They keep going out of the room 'to make adjustments', but really they are in terror of making a psychological leap which they have been taught to think it is not their business to attempt.

174

However, Julliard showed us a play they'd been touring to schools, *In Transit*, a day in the life of the Port Authority Bus Terminal in Manhattan – modern, gritty, vigorous, and very well performed; the Russian students went over the moon about it.

Life at the hotel is looking up. I'm learning to shout at the waiters until they pay attention; I'm getting turned on to Russian Ice Cream, which they serve with elderberries, and is often the only substantial thing on the menu; and I've discovered a classical music station on the radio. On the other hand, I went into my bathroom in the middle of the night, and there were cockroaches on my TOOTHBRUSH.

Also, now that PODIUM is over, there is terrible confusion about our status at the Orlyonok. I tried to sit down for breakfast this morning, and was told 'Problem' by the waiter. Other people, tourists, were munching happily in the half-full dining room. Some of our people have been rung in the middle of the night asking when they were *leaving*. Yesterday, there was no bus; everyone had to hitch a ride into town, missing 40 minutes of classes. This morning the students looked washed out and resentful – they party till all hours, don't sleep, and wonder why they feel ill. The girl from RADA really is ill, I think, and we've sent her to my medical friend at the Embassy. Two of the Americans are quite sick as well, and Eve Shapiro, their Administrator, is hors de combat, so Caroline and I are covering for her.

Honoured Artist Sofia Piliavska, the oldest present member of the Moscow Art Theatre, came to talk to us about Stanislavski and Nemirovitch-Danchenko, under whom she studied. She was fascinating, I think, but as she never allowed her interpreter (a diminutive, moustachioed lady called Alla) to get a word in edgeways, we couldn't be sure.

Lovely lunch chez Gerasimov, Nelly is a wonderful cook; there was a lot of vodka and good Georgian wine, and it went on for about five hours. They have two small rooms and a kitchen/bathroom in a quiet street, and Oleg carefully tends the window-boxes. At 6.30, when Caroline, Natasha and I got unsteadily to our feet, Oleg went straight off to the theatre to rehearse with his own students. Rehearsal hours here have no relation to our own, or any other that I have come across. It is quite common for the Russians to come into the Actors' House for supper after the show, stay drinking and chatting till 2 a.m., and then go off and do a couple of hours rehearsal for a new play.

Jane Hool, the RADA girl, has an acute liver problem. She must be flown home immediately, but there are no flights available. Aeroflot will put her at the head of their standby queue if we can provide a doctor's letter, but the English doctor who saw her is off duty – the Embassy secretary has to find him and get him to write the letter, then we have to get the letter to Aeroflot with her ticket before the office closes at mid-day (it's Saturday). We can't get through to Jane's hotel room to tell her to pack and get ready – hammering on the door produces no response, she's flat out, we cannot make the hotel staff understand the need to open the door and wake her – and all at once the diminutive Alla (be praised) turns up, and accomplishes the whole thing in an hour and a half, speeding around Moscow in a taxi. Two Americans had to go back to Chicago, also genuinely ill, but most of those left (ours too) are looking like death. Any suggestions from me about trying getting enough sleep are liable to be met with sulks.

Dinner with Valery Leventhal, Head of Design at the Bolshoi, and his family. Just as Oleg's apartment was a

176

distinct improvement on Eugene's, this was very different again. High above the ornamental green rooftops, on two floors, with a warren of attic studios above the living quarters, where each of the family paint or sculpt or design. Pamela Howard, who is in Moscow for a few days, took me there; it was quite a big party, and I met some most interesting people, many of them called Sasha.

The next day there was a trip to Zagorsk. I got down punctually to catch the bus, which was to leave at 9.00 to allow us to attend the Cathedral Service at 11.00. The bus actually arrived at 9.50, but didn't leave for another twenty minutes because people had wandered away again. Mark Fisher has joined us (his daughter is one of the two Bristol students), together with two ladies who are friends of John's sound man, and fat Sergei the Bursar from the school, who shouts. Also the girls from the office. It pissed with rain, we got to Zagorsk just as the service ended and they locked the Cathedral, and I got into one of the other smaller churches, packed like sardines with people in steaming mackintoshes, kicking you in the groin to get past and light a candle. Fought for about a quarter of an hour to get out, ten minutes to one, lunch was to be provided at 3. 30, it was still pouring with rain and all the other churches were closed. There's nothing else to do in Zagorsk – I suppose there must have been about two thousand people just standing about, getting wet. I finally managed to pick out our bus among the other thirty-five in the car park, got in, and re-read *Sense and Sensibility*, which for some reason was in the pocket of my raincoat. After two and a half hours, lunch was provided in a sort of refectory. Fat Sergei produced quite a lot of Marsala; an odd choice of beverage, but it warmed my freezing feet and I chatted

177

to Mark Fisher about arts funding problems in that other country that now seems very far away. We then were driven back to Moscow, damp and dissatisfied.

I wanted to go to the Chekhov Vaudeville sketches in the evening, and the bus driver promised to drop me off at a suitable Metro station, but he forgot and went straight to the hotel, so sod it. Want to go *home* now, to hail a taxi that stops, ride in a lift that works, find an art gallery that's open, visit a theatre that's performing what it says it's performing at the time advertised for performing it, go into a restaurant where they'll serve you food. I know I'm being unreasonable, I know the problems of recovering slowly from a bureaucracy that dates back to way before the Revolution – and the fact that I nevertheless still get annoyed about things marks me out as being a mere tourist at heart, which thought of course makes me doubly angry.

Melikhovo
April 1989

Well you see one says these things, and then the next day's wonderful. A sunny, clear, fresh spring day, and we went out to Chekhov's estate here at Melikhovo. It's closed to the public today – Monday – so we were here on our own, by special dispensation. The estate remains completely untouched, even the vegetable garden is still growing produce for the people who look after the estate. We were allowed to film the students rehearsing a couple of scenes from *Vanya* under my direction, inside the house – it all suddenly felt exactly right. Each relationship, every movement took on an authority, a naturalism, that was dictated by the size and shape of the room and the disposition of the furniture. Presumably these were the rooms Chekhov saw in his mind's eye when he wrote his plays – the dining room (*Three Sisters*?) at Melikhovo only just big enough to contain the table; his sister's bedroom (Olga's in the same play?) hung with her paintings, comfortable for one person but no more; his father's room (where Serebriakhov doesn't want to go to bed?) a slim chamber with room only for narrow bed, music stand and chest full of books. What a pity our stages are just too big to be true to the feeling. Bondarchuk got it right in his film of *Vanya.*

Fat Sergei, who has now adopted me as his bosom friend, and comes towards me at intervals with arms outstretched, bellowing 'Timotei! – *wodkaaaa!*', has fixed us all a lovely dejeuner sur l'herbe outside the house on this beautiful still afternoon. Everyone, quite unconsciously, speaks very softly here, moves very gently. I see a knot of students sitting on the grass a little way off, listening, enraptured, to a figure sitting on a hummock in their midst. Who is this adored Guru? Is it the rakish, insouciant Kulyagin, turning his melting brown eyes on each of the prettiest in turn? Or can it be world-weary Gerasimov, carelessly throwing off his dry little epigrams as he knits his brows and lights up yet another yellow cigarette?

But no! It is creaky old BOGOMOLOV, sporting today a light blue jacket and spotted tie, and looking about twenty years younger. He has never been here before, and is having a wonderful time. Under the influence of the sun, the vodka and the idolatrous attentions of his flock, he has blossomed into expansive and melodious rhetoric, and as he tells his tales of the giants of the

179

Russian Theatre who have come and gone, the students liberally top up his glass, and listen spellbound.

Across the grass stands the summer house where *The Seagull* was written, its paint peeling, the putty breaking away from the windows. An old woman works away with an archaic hoe among the lines of young cabbages. A goat is tethered to the fence. There's nothing to tell you it isn't still 1885.

So everyone went home feeling very happy and privileged. Caroline and I were invited back to the school, and into Sergei's office. The walls of his office are lined with metal cupboards, but all these cupboards seem to contain are bottles of vodka wrapped in newspaper, and a lot of curious wafers stuck together with jam, with all of which, however, Sergei was extremely generous. One of the designers was there, and some girls whose business was not explained, and a fierce looking man in a brown suit who may have been a book-keeper – none of them spoke any English, and none of us spoke more than the few words of Russian we'd picked up in three weeks, but it seemed a very good party. Caroline and I walked down to the Rossya for dinner – usual thing, restaurant half empty but we're told it's full. But the waiter asked us if we were French, in what could have been a positive tone; so we decided we were, and talked a lot of French to him, and to each other when he was listening, and we got some dinner. He wasn't French, and didn't speak any, but he obviously liked the nation, and we might try and find him again and repeat the exercise. The trouble is, you never seem to see the same waiter in the same place twice. Is this sinister?

Orlyonok Hotel
April 1989

Apparently Wendy – one of our students – nearly died last night. She and Mark's daughter Fran explored the sisal ski slope in Gorky Park, and in the pitch dark Wendy lost her balance on a slope that had been closed for safety reasons (I suppose there must have been a sign in Kyrilic which she couldn't read) and hurtled downwards towards a tangle of barbed wire. She stopped herself just short of the wire by catching hold of a loose piece of sisal, and Fran managed to talk her back up the steep slope, hand over hand. As if that wasn't enough for one evening, they then went exploring a disused Metro station. I don't know. How many of them will get back to London alive?

Trying to phone Sasha Kulyagin, who has left some very unclear instructions for his students today, reveals the interesting fact that there is no such thing as a telephone directory in Moscow. Even the British Embassy doesn't have the number of the theatre school, or any number, unless someone writes it in a book.

In the afternoon, we went to the famous Turkish Baths. The architecture is a mixture of the Athenaeum and the Randolph Hotel, Oxford. We cavorted about, naked, for the benefit (cinematic, I mean) of John and his camera crew. Lots of supple young bodies – but not mine – plunging into the icy pool. Very refreshing, and

181

afterwards solemn elderly men in white coats bring you tea in a vast, silent, pillared vault.

We made the mandatory pilgrimage to Bulgakov's flat. The stairway leading up to his apartment has been preserved as a sort of shrine; the walls are covered in graffiti – some of them beautifully done – quotes from his works in all languages, pictures of characters, mostly the cat in *The Master and Margharita*, and meetings, attended informally by adherents from all over the world, are held in the courtyard. People are always on the stairs, like us, pointing out their favourite bits of writing. The other residents in the building – I'm told – don't mind at all, they're proud of the association. I kept wondering, mutatis mutandis, how Joe Orton's neighbours might react in similar circumstances.

If, on a scale of 10, Eugene's apartment scored 1, Gerasimov's 3, and the Leventhals' 6 (in this classless society), then Quentin Peel of the Financial Times, at whose flat I dined last night, rates a clear 8. He and his wife, friends of Caroline's, are Irish Catholics, have a number of children and are a lovely family. Wonderful in mid-Moscow to hear the touch of a soft Irish accent, and be offered a Black Bush and sodabread. Delicious dinner (I'm sorry I seem to go on about food, but really anything other than cold sausage and cucumber is such a *treat*), some nice other British journalists and an Irish solicitor with a very tall Chinese wife. It was so cosy that Caroline and I began to feel it was a bit Us and Them, without being quite sure whether, in our peculiar position, we were Us or Them. The wife of the other journalist (they have four children) said that after three years here she loves Moscow, because she doesn't have to make choices. In their position, there's only one place to live, only one school for English-speaking kids, only one doctor for the family, only one place to shop. They're about to be posted to Washington, DC, and she's dreading it.

This morning I had Anatoly Smelyansky back, to talk about the state of modern Russian theatre, with particular reference to the apparent paucity of new writing. He was frank, funny and splendid. He used the image of writers hacking away at the great wall of restriction and censorship erected by Stalin, and maintained with waning conviction by his successors, until Khruschev started discreetly dismantling it brick by brick, checking, each time, for untoward results. By the time Gorbachev took over, the wall was only a few bricks high, but the writers were still lashing out with their picks and sledgehammers at the empty air. 'What are you doing, Comrades?' Smelyansky and his critical colleagues would ask. 'We have to knock down this terrible wall,' would come the reply. 'But look, there no longer is a wall,' the critics reasoned. 'Go away,' cried the writers, 'This is the only thing we know how to do.'

He is a huge success with the students, and is planning a visit to London. You must catch him when he comes.

Mezh Hotel Bar
Mosow
May 1989

Tried to get into a church for Easter Vigil – no chance – but it all looked splendid through a crack in the door, and there was some fine singing. Home on a very festive Metro – it's May Day tomorrow.

Each night there are about a hundred additional cockroaches in the bathroom. Once upon a time I would turn on the overhead light, and they would scurry out of sight in the twinkling of an eye. Now they lounge about or amble gently towards the drain, crossing over to chat to one another on the way. We all have the same experience. Wendy tells me she talks to them, informs them when she wants to have a bath, and they discuss it for a while and then usually withdraw with a good grace.

The May Day decorations, which are splendid, seem to have been magically put up overnight. And here at the smart Mezh Hotel, the Russo-British Exhibition is in full swing. I talked to the Sales Director of a Scottish clothing company about three cashmere scarves which I thought would make perfect presents for the three professors, but the trouble was he wasn't allowed to sell them, he would have to return them through Customs when the Exhibition ends tomorrow. But then the conversation turned to the difficulty of obtaining malt whisky in Moscow, and when I mentioned I had a spare bottle of Glenmorangie back at the hotel, it appeared that we might after all be able to do business. I said I'd be back tomorrow with the inducement.

The British Embassy Cocktail Party, principally in honour of the Exhibition, but to which we had kindly been invited, was fairly magic on account of the beauty of the building and the incredible view from the terrace across the Moscow River, with the setting sun turning the gold of the Kremlin Cathedral minarets first to a burning copper and then to an unearthly dusty red. The guests were mainly the sales staff of the businesses represented, plus their senior management who had come for the ride; these latter were a tightly-knit group, and eyed us, the outsiders, with suspicion and distaste before making up their minds to converse. I would rather have heard about their jobs, but they tended to lead off with : 'My wife says she's seen you on television.' (Subtext: 'though I myself am far too busy for such frivolity'). And then, sternly: 'I have to warn you, I'm not an addict.' ('So if you've wormed your way into this cocktail party hoping for a shower of adulation from serious decent people who frankly couldn't give a toss about your trumpery little TV shows, then the sooner you get back to your cockroaches at the Orlyonok the better.')

However, H.E. is charming – I actually knew his dad, slightly, Warwick Braithwaite, conductor at Sadlers Wells, a great mate of Howell Glynne's. Brian Cox turned up, from London, and took us out to dinner when the party seemed to be running down – not that the running down deterred some of our students, who stayed on to the bitter end and were eventually given soup and tea by the Ambassador and his kind lady, possibly in their pyjamas.

Went to Bogomolov's class next day – his last, I think, with our students. They were rehearsing Nina's last scene in *The Seagull*, where she comes back to say goodbye to the estate, the tattered remains of the theatre in the garden, and to Treplev himself, before going away to take up her first professional job as an actress. I've always thought there was a great sadness in the scene, in that she is saying goodbye to an innocence and perhaps to a little spark of really original talent which is going to die and be forgotten when she becomes a provincial actress – a younger Arkadina, in fact. As we watch, we are not, surely, entirely happy about where her fate is taking her. But Bogomolov was not having this at any price. 'No! this is wonderful!' he cried. 'She is going to be *actress!*' I tried to explain the feelings of misgiving experienced by the average British audience at this point, but this, apparently, is blasphemy. To be an actress is to have a mission in life, a huge responsibility, a cross to

185

carry (Russian vernacular is full of Christian imagery), a destiny to fulfil. Everyone will be envious of her. 'She will be *artist!*'

Of course, what has really been confusing us is that we are at present in a country where acting is considered a valid art form, and where art itself is important.

The class came to an end, and the farewell parties began, all over the building. I looked in on Oleg Gerasimov's final class, he was performing some Ostrovsky for them, wonderfully funny. When it was over, they applauded him to the echo, produced a huge chocolate cake with his name on it, and while he stood behind it all the American girls photographed each other, with him, in turn.

Kulyagin had all his students over to his apartment to watch his film of *Platonov* – I couldn't go as I had to get back to the Mezh to do my scarf deal, but Sasha is apparently quite brilliant in the film, and I'm very sad to have missed out.

I got my scarves, and returned to the Orlyonok to do a lot of present-wrapping before going to the end-of-term party that we ourselves were holding for the Russians – it was a good party, with far too many speeches, but the Russians have a staggering appetite for ceremonial oratory.

Next day at 11 a.m. the Americans left, amid some copious weeping, and as I had the rest of the day to myself I went to the Pushkin Gallery – some very good 18th Century French stuff of various kinds, a few good Picassos and Impressionists; but I did more than ever wish we could have got to Leningrad, to the Hermitage. Even had we had time to go, I gather that getting the necessary travel permit would have taken forever. Had a last wander along the river before going to dinner with

Sue Jameson, who's here as Moscow Correspondent for LBC, at the flat belonging to the Cultural Controller of the British Embassy. (He tops the Apartment League with an undisputed ten out of ten.) Stayed till quite late, and went home on the Metro to pack, for we were leaving next morning.

The Russian students all turned up at the hotel to see us off. And now the car park was absolutely awash with tears. Though perhaps in certain cases the Russian display of emotion might have served an incidental purpose as an acting exercise, most of the individual partings were heartrending to behold, and eyes were still red and swollen when, two hours later, we climbed aboard the Ilyushin for home.

I'm extremely proud of our students – I do think they had a pretty wonderful time, but they also worked incredibly hard and I think learned a tremendous amount. But perhaps the most valuable experience for us all was being made to understand, through our intimacy with the Russians, that national volatility which we seem deeply to mistrust whenever we in Britain attempt their plays. An English actor, finding that he is required to be in a high state of excitement at the bottom of page twenty-six, will commonly turn back the pages of his script until he finds a point, four pages earlier, where he can begin to develop a state of mind that will logically emerge at the required pitch at the required point.

But the Russian comedic character cares nothing for such logic or consistency. He may be sitting at home enjoying his dinner, when he notices that the turnips are under-cooked. All at once the dinner, for him, has lost its attraction. He looks round at his family. In the lamp light somehow they no longer seem the same people on whom he has willingly lavished so much love and care, and for which they now appear grossly ungrateful. He glances out of the window. It is raining hard. Later that evening he has to go out – he will undoubtedly catch cold, and maybe pneumonia. In fact, he will probably die. And will these unsympathetic people sitting round the table really mourn for him? Will they care?

Oh, someone has put a fresh bottle of wine on the table. He tastes it. It is good. It is wonderful wine. How lucky a man is to be sitting at the table in the midst of his family, sharing this excellent repast. And what a fine, dutiful, loving family they are. Was ever man blessed with such a family? And look – out on the estate, the sweet rain is falling! What a harvest it will be! How happy I am! This is the happiest day of my whole life, there is no question about it.

This journey from equanimity to stygian gloom, to rapturous euphoria, may have taken perhaps 45 seconds, and this is how we must learn to play Chekhov.

When I came back from Russia I began work co-producing a play for BBC TV, Blore, MP, *an adaptation of A.N.Wilson's novel* Scandal, *of which I'd purchased the rights. This was about the complicated life of a Cabinet Minister who was in the habit of paying regular visits to a young lady in Southall to have his bottom smacked. About the time it was shown, life was mirroring art so extravagantly that it didn't make much of an impact.*

*The co-production exercise, at all events, was interesting, and taught me a lot. In other ways, too, 1989 was a good year: I got to work with Richard Dreyfuss (*The Price *– BBC Radio), drive a steam locomotive (documentary on the Talyllyn Railway for HTV), and conduct the Halle Orchestra (Beecham, YTV). Who could ask for more?*

Later in the year I went back to Bristol, the city where I spent my boyhood years, attended five schools but was expelled only from one; and where, as a participant in the very first National Student Drama Festival, I was told by Harold Hobson in the gentlemen's lavatory at the Victoria Rooms that I ought to take up the theatre professionally.

Now here I was, playing Solness in The Master Builder *for the Bristol Old Vic Company's new Artistic Director Paul Unwin; and we got on so well that he asked me back for the Autumn 1990 season as his Associate Director – not in fact to direct any plays but to be involved in the policy-making, and to play Lord Ogleby in* The Clandestine Marriage *and* Vanya *in* Uncle Vanya.

189

I imagine the news has reached you already in Australia. Mrs. Thatcher yesterday finally bowed to public opinion, and resigned. Here, no one can talk of anything else. Stella Richman had been thinking about it all through last night's performance of *Vanya*, and at the end of Act IV, instead of saying 'They've gone', said 'She's gone' by accident, and brought the house down.

The headlines this morning defy belief. 'TOO DAMN GOOD FOR THE LOT OF US' (Mail), 'WHAT HAVE THEY *DONE?*' (Express), 'THE FINAL SACRIFICE' (Western Daily Press – our ACU Chaplain regards this one as actionable blasphemy). The Sun simply had 'MRS T-EARS', with a picture of her crying in a car. It's a wonder that the distraught editors could summon the energy actually to bring the papers out.

The Tory politicians have been given a lot of air-time – perhaps a little too much for their own good. Deep grief and simple eulogy were the order of the day, until about half way through 'Newsnight', when tentative criticisms began to nibble at the edges of this blanket of adulation. Gradually more and more people dared to sound a note of dissent. Kenneth Baker, having clearly been caught on the hop by the news, made a few sententious remarks about Party Unity. Douglas Hurd tried to suggest that, if he was in the running as a successor, he wouldn't just be offering a continued form of Thatcherism, but at the same time made it quite clear that he shared no ground with Mr. Heseltine. He found it quite difficult to know what he should say about Mr. Major, as they are supposed to be on the same side, but only up to a point. Tebbitt, a frightened and deserted man, found it hard to be coherent about anyone. Heseltine came out best, refusing to be drawn on the succession, and talking about some trees he was planting that afternoon. Mr. Major was undergoing dental surgery, and unavailable for comment.

A small group of people turned Downing Street into a Wailing Wall, piling the pavement with flowers, and a few people sobbed dutifully into the camera; but now, twenty-four hours later, the situation seems to have been accepted, as W.S. Gilbert said, with an equanimity bordering on indifference.

Anyway, while all this was going on . . . *The Clandestine Marriage* was a huge success, and there is a very good feel about the place at the moment. Audiences for *Vanya* not as good, but then I suppose that's to be expected. They're by no means bad, though, and the critical response has been very favourable. Patrick Malahide follows a hilarious Bristolian Mr. Sterling with a most intelligent Astrov, and Saskia Wickham is very moving as Sonia. Carol Gillies, of course, definitive as old Marina, and her fluent Russian enables us at all times to consult the original text. She is, sadly, not at all well, though we don't know – and she doesn't either – the details of her diagnosis.

Patrick and I were called to the BBC in Whiteladies Road after the show last night for a children's charity Telethon. Five minutes before we were due to go on, we were each given several typewritten sheets of material to learn, but then we hung about till just after midnight, when we were talked to in front of the camera for about thirty seconds. Our interviewer was dressed as a Hungarian peasant, and I only found out later that she was meant to be Russian and we were supposed to make a joke about her working on my estate. No one would have understood anyway.

During the evening's mayhem, one of The Fairer Sax (a brilliant all-woman saxophone consort) had her instrument stolen – hardly surprising since all the street doors seemed to be wide open, not a Commissionaire was to be seen, and a group of very tough looking ten-year-olds were wandering in and out of dressing rooms, dressed as ducks.

Got away from this at a quarter to one, and at eight o'clock this morning we had a Directors' meeting and then I had to open the Castle Park Leisure Area at an Inauguration Ceremony to mark the 50th anniversary of the Blitz which I remember, vividly, watching from my bedroom window in Redland as this part of the city was virtually destroyed overnight.) After the Lord Mayor had referred to me in his speech as Timothy White, and the Parks Superintendent, in his speech, as Peter West, and three people came up to me and asked in surprise what I was doing in Bristol, and I pointed towards the theatre 300 yards away, and they looked baffled, I was quite ready for my lunch. However, I needed to buy some eggs to take back to the flat, and after finding there were no eggs in the Market that morning, I walked round Central Bristol gradually coming to terms with the in-escapable fact that one is not permitted to purchase food in city centres any longer. The Supermarkets are out on a Ring Road somewhere, so if you haven't got a car, tough.

It came on to rain. I wasn't wearing a raincoat. Seeing a Health Food shop, I walked in and asked for some eggs. No, said the girl behind the counter, this is a Health Food shop. I maintained that this didn't exactly answer my question, eggs were *food*, weren't they, was she saying they weren't healthy? No, she said, she wasn't saying that, but they weren't Health Food *as such*. I asked if it were any longer possible to buy eggs anywhere in central Bristol, and she seemed surprised at the question. Not in *central* Bristol, she said, no. Where did I live? Clifton, I told her. She looked at me with a puzzled expression. Why didn't I buy my eggs in Clifton before I came into the city, she asked.

Unsuccessful, lunchless, wet, I made my way back to the theatre for the matinée. I cut through the eggless Baldwin Street Market, and as I passed I heard one stallholder saying to another, 'It's all right for 'im, isn't it? I wouldn't mind being in 'is shoes.'

This was too much. I rounded on the man. 'Look,' I said. 'I got up at first light this morning to attend a meeting in this country's oldest working theatre, to discuss what we are going to do about the fact that your benighted City Council not only cuts our grant steadily from year to year but doesn't even tell us by how *much* until it's too late. I then go and stand in a marquee for an hour while everybody calls me by the wrong name; after which I spend my lunch hour walking around in the rain looking at shops that sell antique firearms, ship's chandllery and custom-made doors but no *food*, and now I've got to go to and do a matinée and an evening show and then go and be gracious to the corporate sponsors at a bunfight afterwards, so don't tell me it's all right for me, and if you'd like to be in my shoes, well here you are, step into them. *All right?'*

The stallholder and his companion looked at me open-mouthed. Then the one who'd spoken raised a hand

and pointed nervously at a third stallholder. 'I was talking about Stuart', he explained humbly.

I collapsed. 'Oh my God I'm *so* sorry,' I gabbled. 'I'm rather overtired, and I haven't been very well, and my wife is in Australia, and I wasn't thinking what I was saying, I do beg your pardon, and yes, I'd like a hundredweight of muesli please, and twelve packets of dried apricots.'

This episode really shook me. I mean, that is *real* paranoia, isn't it. Do you think I ought to seek treatment for it? I mean, do you think I am actually clinically disturbed? Or is that just paranoia on my part?

Pembroke Road
Bristol
December 1990

The financial position here looks gloomier than ever. The City are going to cut us again next year, though Avon County are, admirably, standing firm. The Arts Council are bringing out their hoary old Parity Funding argument again, whereby they match their own contribution to that of the Local Authorities – this was quite sensible at one time, but what with rate-capping, unpaid poll-tax and ever-increasing problems with housing, health and education, even the Councils that feel a strong responsibility towards the arts cannot support them realistically any longer.

Paul has had enough. He is finding, like so many regional Artistic Directors, that the time he should be spending reading plays, seeing plays, going round the country looking at actors, directing and planning, is taken up in endless meetings with the various existing funding bodies and with representatives of the business community, trying to prise out of them some financial support for their historic local theatre.

It *is* an expensive theatre to run, of course. The fabric of any mid-Georgian public building is costly to maintain. And ever since the 1972 technical improvements, audiences have expected a lot in the way of production values; they like *big* shows. The Theatre Royal holds only 650, and of those, as you will remember, 75 seats are useless. We have to keep the prices down – raising them even a little has proved counter-productive – and we need a very high percentage of capacity to get by.

Then there is that other question: Producing Theatre versus Touring Theatre. Ask the average Bristol taxi driver to take you to the Theatre Royal, and he will drive you nine miles to the Theatre Royal Bath. That's where a lot of our erstwhile audience now go. At one time, people used to visit their local Rep once a fortnight, or month, and go on another night to see whatever was on at the big touring house down the street. Two quite different though complementary experiences. Now, as I say, they compete. Fewer people are interested in seeing their local company's version of *Twelfth Night* or *Three Sisters* or *The Country Wife* or *Peer Gynt*, than watching their favourite TV stars on tour in a new (or fairly new) comedy. Bath is a beautifully run theatre, and very pleasant to visit; you can't blame people, it's just that attitudes are changing, and anyway there isn't the money around.

So, in short, Paul is not renewing his contract, and when he goes I shall go too of course. I'm sure he's made the right decision, even though he's got nothing to go on to, and a family to support. To stay would mean increasing frustration, and I think the thing that bugs both of us more than anything else is the present inability to stage any *new* work. We can't budget for the small attendance that new work invariably attracts in the main house, nor can we afford to reopen the Studio. (Incidentally, twelve years ago, the Bristol Old Vic produced 29 plays a year in three auditoria – now we do 8, in one.) What real use is a theatre that cannot do new plays?

I'm sorry to end this rather dismal letter with some more melancholy news. After four weeks, Carol's medical records have been discovered in a hidden file at Hammersmith General Hospital, and the consultant here has ordered her straight in for a biopsy. It looks bad. June Barrie is taking over Marina on Monday.

Oh I'm so looking forward to coming out to join you in Sydney. Christmas Day on the beach, eh, with a pack of Foster's, just like the Poms always imagine it. Can't wait.

The last show I was involved in with the Bristol Old Vic was Eugene O'Neill's Long Day's Journey into Night, *in which Pru and I played Mary and James Tyrone. This was a co-production with the National Theatre, and after leaving Bristol, toured for seven weeks before coming to the Lyttelton stage at the National. It did extremely well in Bristol, and pretty well on tour, but the critics didn't care for Pru and myself in the roles, and in London the audience stayed away in their droves.*

This was followed by a new play of Hugh Whitemore's, It's Ralph, *at the Comedy. This time the notices were quite good, but a combination of the recession, fog, IRA bombings and someone bringing the Southern Region railway system to a standstill by setting fire to the signal box at London Bridge, ensured that nobody came to see that either.*

I was invited to Dublin by my friend Alan Stanford to play King Lear *for his Second Age Company there. It would be the first Shakespeare play I had done in twelve years, so I accepted with alacrity.*

Clonskeagh
Dublin
October 1992

Well, King Lear again, eh. Twenty years since the end of the last one. And forty years since I did it at school. Perhaps in another twenty years' time, when I'm nearer the right age, I'll be allowed to do it again somewhere. As it is, I feel I already know more about it than last time. In 1971, the boys were only tiny, now, they're of an age when both they and I must harbour occasional thoughts of the nuisance I may be to them in my dotage. Would you say I'm a more selfish, certainly a more intolerant person than I was twenty years ago? I expect you would. Well, sorry, tough, the first two acts seem to be the better for it. Jonathan Miller is here, rehearsing *The Double Dealer* for the Gate, and is being very helpful to me on the medical history.

Alan's directing it very well, I think. He's good on text, sound on the psychological development, knows his theatre, and has a refreshingly low boredom threshold. A talented cast, that bats all the way down, and are a pleasure to be with. I'm enjoying myself very much, and have been given a rent-free four-bedroomed house here on the way out to Blackrock; I sleep on each of the six beds in turn.

Perhaps the most worthwhile aspect of the exercise is that very few people in Dublin have ever seen the play before. Very little Shakespeare is done here, in fact. They of course pay more attention than we do to the other Standard English Playwrights like Farquhar, Congreve, Sheridan, Goldsmith, Wilde, Shaw and Beckett – who were all Irish or part-Irish anyway, whereas Shakespeare wasn't. Dubliners will courteously muse with you upon this curious anomaly, being too polite to point out that producing Shakespeare here is a bit like draping the stage with the Union Jack. But it is studied in schools – hence Alan's company, which has a special responsibility to cater for schools audiences from all over the country.

When I first caught sight of the Tivoli Theatre – where we open in a fortnight – my heart sank. It's in that bit of Dublin they call the Liberties, up the hill past the Castle and the Protestant Cathedral, where the markets are; and looks derelict. Opposite, rough timber props are holding up a crumbling pub. The street is unlit, and deep in refuse from the market stalls. Inside, the decor is austere, but the basic layout of the place rather exciting, and ideal for our purposes. There is a thrust stage, deeper than it is wide, with the bulk of the audience on tiered seating in front and about four rows either side of the stage. The acoustics are excellent, the dressing rooms and wardrobe wonderfully tatty, but there appears to be warmth, and there is a shower that works.

I've seen a good *Tartuffe* at the Gate, and a pretty splendid *Iceman* at the Abbey, full of wonderful Irish character acting. I'm striking off across Ireland to Mayo and Achill at the weekend – tell you about it in my next letter.

Tivoli Theatre
Dublin
November 1992

On the island of Achill at this time of year, all the hotels and boarding houses, and all the bed-and-breakfasts, are closed. However, the Irish Tourist Office, deeply intrigued by the idea of anyone wanting to go to the West Coast in this weather (howling wind and rain), rose to the challenge and came up with a Mrs. Halloran at Achill Sound, who telephoned to say she would expect me at some time on Saturday night.

It was a long drive, across the rather dull central part of the country, and night was falling when I got up to Newport Bay with its hundreds of tiny atolls, and the Nephin Beg Mountains rising to the north. So by the time I got to the island causeway it was pitch dark, with the rain beating against the windscreen. Nobody about, and very difficult to find Mrs. Halloran. However, I eventually identified the lane she lived in, and by slewing the car athwart the road outside each house and shining the headlights on the gateposts, I eventually made out the letters 'B&B'. I got out, tramped up the dark drive and rang the bell.

The door was opened by a witch. No, I mean a real witch, a fairy tale witch, four feet high with a hooked nose, blackened teeth and a wispy beard, and a tall pointed hat. I started back in alarm. At this the witch laughed, and then rather surprisingly called out for her mother, because this was Mrs. Halloran's twelve-year-old daughter, and it was Hallowe'en, which I'd forgotten. Hallowe'en is very big here, and for the rest of the evening small groups of children came knocking on the door with herbs for Mrs. Halloran, who gave them cake and a few coins, and they sang her songs, in Gaelic.

Mrs. Halloran was going to a ceilidhe in the village later in the evening, and asked if I'd like to come. I said it was kind of her, but I really just wanted to spend a quiet evening reading a book. She apologised for the fact that she couldn't give me anything to eat, but told me that if I took the car back across the causeway, I could buy some eggs and rashers at the post office at Rosfurk and bring them home and cook them on her stove, which I did.

The next morning the storm had blown itself out, and it was a beautiful crisp, clear day. I explored the island, stopping at a tiny chapel on the sea shore around which lay the graves of the island victims of the potato famine in the eighteen forties. There were an awesome number of gravestones, and I noticed that some of the later ones were quite roughly hewn and inexpertly engraved. Then it struck me that of course stone masons were no more immune from the disaster than anyone else. I went for a long walk, and then drove back along the coast road to Castlebar for a pie and a Guinness, and thence to Galway City.

The Great Southern Hotel is an old railway hotel, very grand once upon a time and still very pleasant in its faded gentility – huge mahogany wardrobes, marble-topped washstands; very old, attentive and loquacious waiters. I've never been to Galway before, it's very attractive, very French; little steep alleyways, candle-lit bistros with check tablecloths, people sitting playing chess. Nothing on at the Druid Theatre, of course, being Sunday, and indeed the building looked pretty dead – I don't know who's got it now that Gary Hines has gone to the Abbey.

But the rest of the town was swinging – I found a nice bar for a chat and had a good dinner, and happily to bed.

Next morning I drove back to Dublin slowly as I wasn't rehearsing, through Athlone, which has not much to commend it, and Meath. I bought a bag of peat blocks, lit a fire and settled down to watch television. Dublin is cabled up for BSkyB, and with the two RTE channels and Ulster TV and BBC 1&2, that makes about eight or nine channels in all; and it is interesting the difference this makes to people's general conversation in the morning, in shops or at the bus stop. The difference, I mean, between Dublin and London, where, broadly speaking, there are still only two widely-watched channels, so that what they showed last night becomes a natural staple of conversation. Here, because everyone is watching something different, nobody talks about it. It obviously doesn't matter here, since conversation for the Irish is never a problem; but in England, once we get a proliferation of cable and satellite choices offered us, a certain conventional social bonding, which may be valuable, will be lost.

Tivoli Theatre
Dublin
November 1992

The costumes were a bit of a shock. We have a Japanese designer, who in fact is very clever; but we didn't see any drawings – or indeed any designer – until the very last moment, when some adjustments had hastily to be made to accommodate what the actors had actually been doing in rehearsal for three weeks. The design inspiration is from Kurusawa's film *Ran*. This is Also Ran. But it works pretty well – for the chaps, anyway; the girls' stuff is less successful, I feel, but not objectionable.

It's been very well received, but it's rather alarming how few adults can actually get to see the show – the schools have practically booked us out. They mostly behave very well, though of course you get the odd ones, but I question the value of bringing kids to a theatre where they form 80 per cent of the audience. They're not coming, or shouldn't be, just to get help with their exams – it should also be an introduction to theatre-going, and that means seeing what it's like to sit for two and a half hours watching a play, surrounded by adults who you don't know. If they limited the schools element to 25 per cent, I think that might be all right, but the demand has been so great that we'd need, in that case, to run for three months. Some of them come all the way from Donegal – they won't get home till 2.30 in the morning.

They are thrilled by the play, though, mostly, and so I think are the adults on the nights when we don't allow the schools in (though what can we do if somebody rings up to book a party of twenty-six, and when they get here they turn out to be schoolchildren?)

No, the only thing that' s been a bother are the digital alarms. In the natural course of things, 'Thou'lt come no more; never, never, never, never, never', the quietest moment of the play, must occur at exactly eleven o'clock. To avoid it being drowned out by seventy five different chiming wristwatches, I do a quick calculation just before I carry Cordelia on for my last entrance; if we're running a bit late, I slow down the early part of the scene so as to get the pips in before the quiet bit, and if we're a little ahead, I get a move on so that they go off during Edgar's final speech, which he hates.

You shouldn't really have to think about that, though, should you, when you're playing King Lear?

POSTSCRIPT

Well, I have to stop somewhere, and this seems as good a place as any. The reader, if he or she is still with me, has been trudging along now for thirty-one years, and I think that is enough for anybody.

These letters span a generation, in the sense that our son Samuel West, also an actor, was the same age by the end of this book as I was at the beginning. How have things changed in those thirty-one years? What advantages have Sam and his contemporaries to look forward to, and what have they missed out on?

On the credit side obviously there's the National Theatre, with its three auditoria. The RSC has increased its performance spaces from two to five since 1961. The Almeida and the Donmar Warehouse now fill an important gap that existed between the smaller fringe theatres and the major subsidised houses.

BBC2 and Channel 4 have grown up in the meantime, both of whom still make, or buy in, good drama. There will be plenty of alternative television too, cable and satellite, and while their dramatic output will probably be negligible, they will indirectly provide a lot of employment in commercials and voice-overs, useful to pay the mortgage and perhaps subsidise eight weeks in Sheffield or Southampton to do an interesting play.

Thirty years ago, although we used to record plays on to disc or tape, we didn't do novels. Now, however,

Talking Books represent a rapidly growing field of employment (personally I love it. It's like casting a play yourself and then playing all the parts). And, thank God, there is still Radio. Though the actual hours of drama per week may have been reduced, what's left is in many ways more adventurous than it was in the sixties.

Nevertheless, re-reading these letters, I'm rather shocked to find that so many of the things I was writing about simply don't exist any more. Classical touring, for instance. The purpose of the Prospect/Old Vic Company was to provide this service full-time, and when the company went to the wall, that task was taken on by the English Shakespeare Company and by Compass Theatre, both of whom produced high-quality work, and both of whom suffered the same fate as the Old Vic through withdrawal of funds. Since then, the UK has had no large-scale classical touring company as such.

Overseas touring is the same. If you're a five-person group, and one of you plays the guitar and drives the mini-bus, the British Council budget might accommodate you, but the days when we used to go round the Middle East with a company of twenty-five or thirty people are long gone.

The superiority of the present regional producing theatres (perhaps the most vital element of theatrical activity in this country) over the old weekly and fortnightly reps, has been achieved at a price. They obviously don't do so many plays, and they don't, except in a very few instances, carry permanent companies. These may seem minor considerations, but in the early sixties, a young actor by the end of a year in a good rep might well have come to grips with Shakespeare, Congreve, Molière, Ibsen, Chekhov, Wilde, Coward and Shaw, as well as Agatha Christie. No doubt a lot of the time we were terrible – the production photos from those days make one blush, especially for the make-up – but we did *do* the plays, and no one gets that practical training any more.

In the world of television, there have been profound recent changes which suggest that we have seen the best of our times. Is the embattled and accountant-driven BBC likely to come up with another Shakespeare Canon? (Whatever you may have thought of some of the individual results, it was a remarkable and proper thing to attempt). Another *Churchill and the Generals* or *Monocled Mutineer*? I'm drawing examples only from my very limited direct involvement. ITV gave us *Edward VII* in the 70's. But since then there have been the Broadcasting Act, the franchise auction, and now the Network Centre – an organisation that has recently sprung up to dictate not only what we see on commercial television, but how it is written and even *cast*, according to the supposed wishes of the advertisers. A casual glance through the Radio Times doesn't suggest to me that all this has been an influence for good.

I notice also how *people* have changed – colleagues, people in the business. And me. Like teachers and doctors, if we're interested in the survival of our profession, we've had to become businessmen. We sit on committees, we attend fund-raising meetings, lobby MPs, read endless balance-sheets, become trustees of this and governors of that. Is this entirely a good thing? It has, I hope, helped to subvert the popular conviction that theatre people are by definition feckless beings consumed with a desire to ruin the economy; but I wonder if it doesn't perhaps sap too much of the energy we should be applying elsewhere, and indeed, whether we use it as an excuse for not doing so.

Sam seems to us to belong to a highly talented generation of new actors, and the opportunities for those who have managed to put themselves on the map at an early age must be very exciting. Analysis of the present cinema audience shows the important market to aim at to be the eighteen to twenty-eight-year-olds, who naturally want to see films about their contemporaries. The responsibility that I think our young actors and actresses must shoulder now, is getting audiences of that age back into the *theatre*. For we have virtually lost that generation, partly through the withdrawal of school visits to the theatre, the cutting of TIE companies, theatrical outreach resources and fit-up tours, but most of all through the closure of second auditoria at regional theatres, which the younger people used to patronise in understandable reaction against what they viewed as the staid, middle-aged, parental audience in the main house.

Recently, I was doing a new play at the Nuffield Theatre, Southampton, which is situated within the University campus, and across the lawn from the refectory. I was sitting having a cup of tea one afternoon, and got into conversation with one of the lecturers from the University's Film Department. She'd seen me in something on television recently, and asked me what I was doing in Southampton. I pointed across the grass to the theatre, and said I was in a play. 'Do you never go to the theatre?' I asked her. She said no. I felt entitled to push her a bit. 'But our film industry,' I said, 'unlike Hollywood, has its roots in the theatre. Don't you ever feel like dropping in, out of curiosity?' No. 'What about your students?' I asked. 'Do they ever go?' 'Oh no,' she replied firmly. 'They're all quite young.'

You see.

The *next* thirty years will be very interesting indeed.

TW, March 1994